POCKET
PRECINCTS

MONTRÉAL
& QUÉBEC CITY

A pocket guide to the cities's best
cultural hangouts, shops, bars
and eateries

PATRICIA MAUNDER

Hardie Grant
TRAVEL

CONTENTS

INTRODUCTION

Bienvenue à Montréal! Welcome to Montréal!

Neither French nor English, or even typically Canadian, cosmopolitan, effortlessly bilingual Montréal is the largest city in the French-speaking province of Québec. While the provincial capital, Québec City, makes the world swoon with its centuries-old heritage charm, Montréal is more about what's happening now. When's the next design market in this UNESCO City of Design? Who are the Habs playing in the hockey? What's on tap at the local brewpub? Who's headlining at the world's biggest jazz and comedy festivals? What's in season at the farmer's markets?

Of course, a city established in 1642 has history to explore too. There was more than a century of French rule. Another century under the British, when it became an international Industrial Revolution powerhouse. Then a Canadian metropolis, wrestling with its mixed-heritage past but mostly getting on with living life to the full, including with migrants from around the globe. And with visitors, especially during Expo '67 and the 1976 Olympics – whose daring main stadium remains a symbol of the city.

Its eternal symbol is Mont Royal, the big hill that gave Montréal its name. This seasonally evolving backdrop is a favourite playground in a town that loves getting outside – especially in summer. The festival season hots up, and everyone living in the inner-city's distinctive apartments gets out on their balconies and beyond, to parks, bike paths and the outdoor seating, the terrasses, of bars and restos – shorthand for restaurants here.

Discover where Montréalais are eating and drinking, from the emerging craft cocktail bars to the best places for the city's holy trinity of fast food: poutine, bagels and smoked-meat sandwiches. Find out why it's Canada's cultural capital, from museums and galleries to architecture, projections and street art. Or explore the new neighbourhoods of cool in Montréal – aka MTL.

Then travel east on a field trip to Québec City, north to Mont Tremblant where adventure awaits, and west to Canada's capital, Ottawa – if you can drag yourself away from Montréal.

Patricia Maunder

A PERFECT MONTRÉAL DAY

The ultimate way to start the day is with Montréal-style bagels – and you can eat them any time because **St-Viateur Bagel**, in the Plateau-Mont-Royal, is open 24/7. If it's not too early, check out **Aux 33 Tours**' records, **Tresnormale**'s tees or the **Drawn & Quarterly** bookshop, then walk up Mont Royal for city views from **Kondiaronk** lookout. Head back down through urban wilderness, and take in art old and new, local and international, at the **Musée des Beaux-Arts de Montréal** (Montréal Museum of Fine Arts).

Then catch the Métro and explore an inner precinct like the reborn Les Quartiers du Canal, where **Atwater Market**'s gourmet food becomes a picnic by the **Lachine Canal**, or a boozy lunch on **McAuslan** brewery's terrasse segues into drooling over **Vintage Frames Company** eyewear. In Little Italy, lunch at **Jean Talon Market**, then shop for made-in-Montréal gifts at **Tah-Dah!** and cocktail gear at **Alambika** before espresso at old school **Caffè Italia**. Or discover up-and-coming Hochelaga-Maisonneuve, lunching at retro **Atomic Café** and finding unique treasures at **Coccinelle Jaune** and **Kitsch à l'os … ou pas**. Come this way at some point for a closer look at the iconic 1976 **Olympic Stadium** and a **Jardin Botanique** wander – especially if Gardens of Light is on.

Head back into town for crazy good times at **La Ronde** amusement park or the **Saute Moutons** Lachine Rapids jet boat ride. Prefer to relax? Do it in style at **Bota Bota** floating spa. Then indulge in Montréal's love for cinq à sept (drinks and snacks, from 5 to 7pm) on the **Terrasse Nelligan** rooftop, where Old Montréal's architecture is on show. Stroll around this historic precinct, including **Notre-Dame Basilica**, before dinner. For a special occasion, make it **Toqué!** Or stick with snacks, like **Queues de Castor**'s pastries, while enjoying **Cité Mémoire** projections, outdoor festival fun and the international fireworks competition.

Then party in the Latin Quarter and The Village. Cocktails at **Renard** and a drag show at **Mado**? Rum and Haitian bites at **Agrikol** or craft beer and poutine at **Le Saint-Bock**? In the wee hours, especially if you still haven't tried poutine, go to the best in town at **La Banquise**, which is open 24/7.

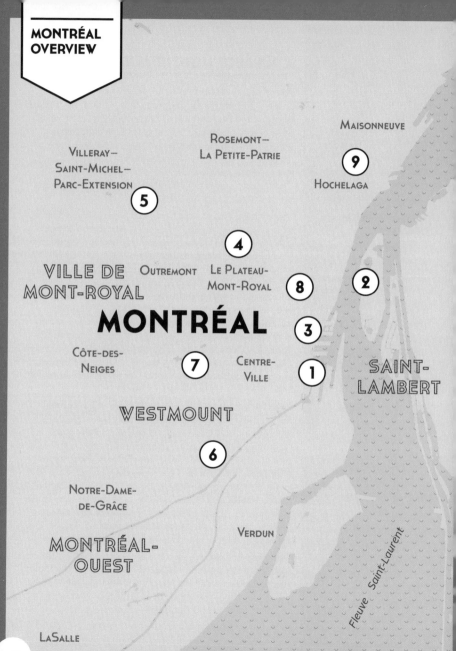

MONTRÉAL
OVERVIEW

MAISONNEUVE

ROSEMONT–
LA PETITE-PATRIE

VILLERAY–
SAINT-MICHEL–
PARC-EXTENSION

(9)

HOCHELAGA

(5)

(4)

VILLE DE
MONT-ROYAL

OUTREMONT

LE PLATEAU–
MONT-ROYAL

(8)

(2)

MONTRÉAL

(3)

CÔTE-DES-
NEIGES

(7)

CENTRE-
VILLE

(1)

SAINT-
LAMBERT

WESTMOUNT

(6)

NOTRE-DAME-
DE-GRÂCE

VERDUN

MONTRÉAL-
OUEST

Fleuve Saint-Laurent

LASALLE

CAPITALE-
NATIONALE

**QUÉBEC
CITY**
(10)

MAURICIE

CHAUDIÈRE-
APPALACHES

LANAUDIÈRE

(11)

CENTRE-DU-
QUÉBEC

LAURENTIDES

(12) **MONTRÉAL**

ESTRIE

MONTÉRÉGIE

PRECINCT∫

FIELD TRIP∫

OLD MONTRÉAL

One of North America's oldest urban areas, this precinct by the Saint Lawrence River is where Montréal began in 1642 when the first French settlers arrived. After a precarious start, this patch of New France prospered, then thrived as a trading and financial centre after the British took over in 1760 and the Industrial Revolution kicked in. Though a few French buildings remain, most date from this boom period – which ended with the Great Depression. With most heritage saved through neglect, it was reborn as historic Montréal's favourite tourist area.

Visitors love the cobblestone streets, centuries-old architecture, grand statues and, until the end of 2019, the horse-drawn carriages (banned due to animal welfare concerns). If you can handle or avoid the crowds, which get crazy during summer, Old (Vieux) Montréal is picturesque, fascinating and charming (and would be more so with fewer cars). Explore or just relax amid the sound of church bells and good times, ideally on a terrasse. As soon as it's warm, these outdoor spaces for eating, drinking and watching are everywhere in Montréal. Some of the city's best are high up, and, for views alone, Old Montréal has the ultimate rooftop terrasses.

Métro stations: Champ-de-Mars, Place d'Armes.

↦ *French colonial style at Old Montréal's annual 18th-century market*

SIGHTS
1. Pointe-À-Callière
2. Notre-Dame Basilica
3. Cité Mémoire

SHOPPING
4. Petite Maison Bleue par Hatley

SHOPPING & EATING
5. Maison Pepin
6. Délices Érable & Cie

EATING & DRINKING
7. Terrasse Nelligan
8. Toqué!
9. Olive + Gourmando

DRINKING
10. The Coldroom

1 POINTE-À-CALLIÈRE

350 Place Royale
514 872 9150
www.pacmusee.qc.ca
Open Mon–Fri 10am–6pm,
Sat–Sun 11am–6pm (summer);
other seasonal hours vary.
[MAP p. 165 D4, 166 C1]

Walk among layers of history at this museum on the spot where the first French colonists arrived and built a settlement, on land that became known as Pointe-à-Callière when Governor Callière's residence was constructed here in 1695. From 17th-century graves to a grand 19th-century insurance building's hefty foundations, you can see several archaeological sites. A major extension in 2017, Montréal's 375th anniversary, means it's now possible to walk along a cut-stone sewer, which covered over the Petite Saint-Pierre River in 1832, to a section of the original fortified settlement's foundations. Centuries of artefacts are displayed, including precious objects made by First Nations peoples long before the French arrived. Don't miss the *Yours Truly, Montréal* multimedia show, which covers the Ice Age to now. Pop up to the museum's tower lookout for great views.

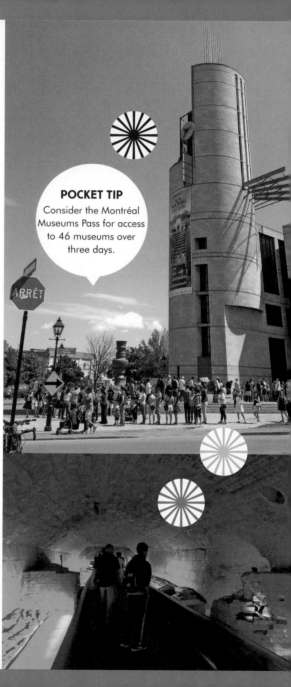

POCKET TIP
Consider the Montréal Museums Pass for access to 46 museums over three days.

2 NOTRE-DAME BASILICA

110 Rue Notre-Dame Ouest
514 842 2925
www.basiliquenotredame.ca
Open Mon–Fri 8am–4.30pm,
Sat 8am–4pm, Sun 12.30pm–
4.30pm, Aura show at various
times.
[MAP p.164 C3]

This is among the 'New World's' most memorable churches, especially the sky-blue vaulted ceiling strewn with 24-carat gold stars. If you're into art, design and heritage, pay the modest entry fee, which includes an optional guided tour. The church built here in 1672 by priests of the Sulpician order was replaced by the current, much larger one in 1843. Today, the slightly stern grey-stone exterior is dramatically lit at night, and the opulent altarpiece, stained glass and lavish gold decoration are always impressive. See *Aura*, a show of music, light, lasers and projections that makes the art and interior come alive. Don't bother queueing before it starts because everyone wanders inside freely for the pre-show's animated artworks. The basilica adjoins the original Sulpician seminary, Montréal's oldest building. You can see the facade, including the 1701 clock, from the street (or courtyard if the gate's open).

POCKET TIP

Entry is free at nearby Notre-Dame-de-Bon-Secours Chapel, where model ships donated by pious sailors of old hang from the ceiling.

3

3 CITÉ MÉMOIRE

Various locations
www.montrealenhistoires.com/
en/cite-memoire
Seasonal schedule

Unlike a traditional walking tour, discover the city's history through Montréal en Histoire (Montréal in stories), a fun, free app that uses virtual and augmented reality. The experience is enhanced at night as you see the Cité Mémoire video projections that bring centuries of history to life on walls around Old Montréal in particular. It takes you from Place d'Armes' open space and gracious architecture to little alleys that are a bit grimey but safe. Plug headphones into your device and you also get music and story narration – from how the city's first executioner was a soldier guilty of 'a crime against nature' and preferred the job to the death penalty, to the memories of an official hostess at the Expo '67 world fair. The biggest production is the twice nightly Grand Tableaux, a towering video projection of Montréal's history, behind city hall. The Cité Mémoire schedule is most frequent June to August but starts later as sunset is close to 9pm in mid-summer. Public guided tours around the projections are limited to May to September, but private ones are available all year.

4 PETITE MAISON BLEUE PAR HATLEY

350 Rue Saint-Paul Est,
shop 264, Marché Bonsecours
building
514 798 6755
www.hatley.com
Open daily 10am–6pm
[MAP p.165 E2]

If you want to take home some fun Canadian souvenirs, the Hatley brand has got you covered, from socks to boxers, baby onesies to kidult pyjamas. This family business began in 1986 in the quaint town of North Hatley, just east of its eventual HQ in Montréal. Artist Alice Oldland painted some aprons with farmyard animals, which were a hit at her Little Blue House gift shop and soon led to the signature cartoon-cute Canadian animals, sometimes with silly puns too. Clothes are the main draw, including a big children's range, but there are also homewares like mugs, oven mitts and descendants of those original aprons. Mine is still in great shape after six years of kitchen action with no sign of the bear wielding a baguette and wine bottle fading or cracking. Whether it's these 'Cabearnet' aprons, moose-print adult onesies with bum flaps or something more subdued in classic red-and-black plaid, Hatley is Canadian for adorable.

POCKET TIP
Find gourmet goodies at Le Petit Dep, a charming, vintage-style convenience store (dépanneur).

5 MAISON PEPIN

378 Rue Saint-Paul Ouest
514 844 0114
www.thepepinshop.com
Open Mon–Sat 10am–6pm,
Sun 11am–5pm
[MAP p. 166 B2]

In this big heritage industrial space of rough grey-stone walls and wooden ceiling beams is an eclectic gathering of objects, often designed and made locally. Find Tungstène's handmade lamps and light fittings – industrial vintage that exudes 21st-century minimalist style. Or WYNIL's wallpapers, Ramacieri Soligo's tiles and artist and owner Lysanne Pepin's own creations, including tassels and scented candles. Her creative eye oversees everything, from product selection to interior style. Linger at the in-store cafe operated by artisanal local bakery business **L'Amour du Pain** (love of bread). While enjoying simple fare like coffee, pastries and sandwiches, consider what to take home – there's plenty of luggage-sized options, such as skincare and cushion covers. Or step along to the (mostly women's) fashion boutique **Espace Pepin** a few doors down, also curated by Madame Pepin. An easy, timeless aesthetic weaves through everything, from blouses to boot and bags.

6 DÉLICE/ ÉRABLE & CIE

84 Rue Saint-Paul Est
514 765 3456
www.deliceserableetcie.com
Open daily 10am–11pm
(summer); other seasonal
hours vary.
[MAP p. 165 D3]

Did you know Québec
produces three-quarters of the
world's maple syrup? For the
guaranteed good stuff and an
array of other maple products,
head to Délices Érable & Cie
(Maple Delights & Co). It's a
retail store for the century-
old Citadelle Maple Syrup
Producers' Cooperative, whose
members tap sap from seven
million maple trees and boil
it down into unadulterated
liquid gold. At this bright, sleek
boutique-cafe, you can buy
different grades, from the early
season's golden, delicately
flavoured style to late season's
dark, robust drop. There are
functional bottles and beautiful
bottles, including maple-leaf-
shaped ones and flasks with
an elegant pewter maple-leaf
decoration. Other temptations
include maple popcorn, maple
tea, maple butter, candy, sugar,
nuts and dressings, plus treats
to enjoy in-store including
maple ice-cream and cookies.
Cranberry and honey products
have been added lately,
making the sweet shopping
quandary harder.

POCKET TIP
If everything's eaten
before you make it
to the airport, don't
worry, there's another
Délices Érable & Cie
store there.

7 TERRASSE NELLIGAN

5th floor, 106 Rue Saint-Paul
Ouest
514 788 4021
www.terrassenelligan.com
Open May–Sept Mon–Fri
11.30am–11pm, Sat–Sun
10.30am–11pm
[MAP p. 165 D4]

After extensive research,
I've concluded that this is
the very best rooftop terrasse
in Old Montréal. Here you
can get an eyeful of the
19th-century **Notre-Dame
Basilica** (*see* p. 3) and the
100-metre (328 foot) 1931
Art Deco **Aldred building**.
Look the other way, across
the Saint Lawrence River:
there's Habitat 67, the striking
modernist apartment complex
reminiscent of precariously
piled toy blocks. What more
could you want? Perhaps the
lobster rolls and some chilled
rosé. From waffles for brunch
to wagyu burger for dinner,
plus summery cocktails,
it's all about indulgence. A
fashionable party vibe builds
in peak season, but prices
aren't over the top. Heaters
and retractable awnings
ward off unpleasant weather,
though not enough to extend
the season outside May
to September.

POCKET TIP
Hôtel Nelligan's year-round
wining and dining options
downstairs may lack the
rooftop terrasse's bubbly
alfresco mood, but October
to April in Montréal is all
about getting cosy.

8 TOQUÉ!

900 Place Jean-Paul-Riopelle
514 499 2084
www.restaurant-toque.com
Open Tues–Fri 11.30am–
1.45pm, Tues–Thurs 5.30–
10pm, Fri–Sat 5.30–10.30pm
[MAP p. 164 B4, 166 A1]

If you have only one extravagant meal in Montréal, Toqué! is the place. It's consistently first or second on the industry-voted Canada's 100 Best Restaurants list. Head chef since it opened in 1993, Normand Laprise has led the way in seasonal, local produce-driven dining in Québec. He's pioneered playful juxtapositions like halibut and raspberry meat jus, on plates with refined creativity: a swirl of sauce, a dollop of foam, beautiful colours, shapes and textures. Fresh regional produce, from lobster to mushrooms, is obvious in every bite. Sommelier Carl Villeneuve-Lepage, who placed third in the 2018 Best Sommelier of the Americas, features Québec beer and wine in the European-focused drinks list. You'll dine in understated contemporary luxury with wine bottles suspended from the ceiling above the cellar, white tablecloths, plush carpet and subdued shades of purple, red and orange. Treat yourself, even if it's just one course at the informal bar.

9 OLIVE + GOURMANDO

351 Rue Saint-Paul Ouest
514 350 1083
www.oliveetgourmando.com
Open daily 8am–6pm
[MAP p.166 B2]

If the entrance counter artfully loaded with baked goods doesn't get you salivating, best check your pulse. From almond croissants to chocolate brownies, they taste even better than they look. No wonder, because co-owner Dyan Solomon was head pastry chef at Toqué! (*see* p. 12) before she opened Olive + Gourmando in 1998 with Éric Girard, a fellow alumni from Montréal's most acclaimed restaurant. The rustic goodness at their bakery soon morphed into this even more popular cafe. Sweet treats complement a compact menu of dishes made with quality ingredients and a homestyle touch. Fresh, inventive salads make healthy eating a joy, and essentials like bread, ricotta and granola are handmade. The hot and cold sandwiches could be the best in town. Seriously, is there a better grilled cheese than their take with caramelised onion, raclette and aged gouda? Arrive before midday for any chance of a lunchtime seat, let alone a table, and good luck on weekends. Luckily most of the menu is good to go.

POCKET TIP
Try *sabrage*, the old French method of opening Champagne with a short sabre, at Vieux Montréal's La Champagnerie bar.

10 THE COLDROOM

155 Rue Saint-Paul Est (rear)
514 451 6911
www.thecoldroommtl.com
Open daily 5pm–3am
[MAP p. 165 D3]

Montréal's fledgling craft cocktail scene took flight in 2016 when this basement bar opened in an old industrial cold storage room. There were already a few joints with obscure entrances, but this one took it to the next level with no signage and, until word got out, no known address. Adding to its audacity is the location amid Old Montréal's tourist traps. Entry is speakeasy-style: although it's on Rue Saint-Paul Est, press the buzzer by the unremarkable black door on the dogleg laneway corner of Saint-Amable and Saint-Vincent streets (look for the little white duck icon), and hope there's room while you wait. Good to go? Follow the gatekeeper down the stairs into this dimly lit 19th-century space of exposed red-brick walls and low wooden beams, refreshed with a contemporary lick. The cocktails are old-school-meets-new with twists on classics like the Martinez, and smart seasonal offerings that maintain the same standards of traditional techniques and quality ingredients, from spirits and bitters to fresh fruits.

THE OLD PORT & PARC JEAN-DRAPEAU

Welcome to Montréal's playground – at its heart, on the Saint Lawrence River. Sandwiched between this massive river and Old Montréal, the Old Port was reinvented after port activities relocated in 1978. Today it's about pleasure, like the Tyrolienne MTL Zipline (*see* p. 23), Bota Bota floating spa (*see* p. 20) and sightseeing cruises. More plans for play are afoot, including turning the port's heritage grain silos into condos, bars and restaurants. From here, take a ferry to the close-by islands of Sainte-Hélène and Nôtre-Dame, collectively known as Parc Jean-Drapeau. You'll find La Ronde amusement park (*see* p. 22) and striking structures built for the Expo '67 world fair: an iconic geodesic dome (now the Biosphère environment museum) and the French and Québec pavilions (now Montréal's casino). The park's playlist goes from the Grand Prix and Osheaga music festival (at a new 65,000-seat natural amphitheatre from 2019, all going to plan), to cross-country skiing. In this city in search of a beach, there's also a lakeside faux beach, Plage Jean-Doré, and another in the Old Port, Plage d'Horloge. The port and park can be bleak when it's cold, though the Fête des neiges winter festival, Igloofest dance parties and outdoor skating are cool fun.

Métro stations: Parc Jean-Drapeau, Champ-de-Mars, Place d'Armes

→◄ *The Biosphère*

THE OLD PORT &
PARC JEAN-DRAPEAU

1 STEWART MUSEUM

20 Chemin du Tour-de-l'Isle,
Parc Jean-Drapeau
514 861 6701
www.stewart-museum.org
Open Tues–Sun 10am–5pm
(summer); other seasonal
hours vary
[MAP p.169 B3]

In the 1820s, after Britain
almost lost its Canadian
territory to the Americans in
the War of 1812, His Majesty's
army constructed a fort
complex on Île-Saint Hélène.
Several buildings remain,
most notably the arsenal,
now home to this quietly
fascinating history museum
about European influence
in the region. Exploration,
science, military matters and
religion are the focus of its
27,000 artefacts – including
the canons outside. The
permanent exhibition, 'History
and Memory', covers five
centuries through 500 objects,
like maps with hazy ideas
about North America and
a super-sized model of an
18th-century ship. Another
highlight is the interactive
model of Montréal prior to the
demolition of its fortifications
in the early 19th century. Take
a wander to find Fort de l'Île
Sainte-Hélène's other restored
buildings; the larger of the two
powder magazines is almost
a secret.

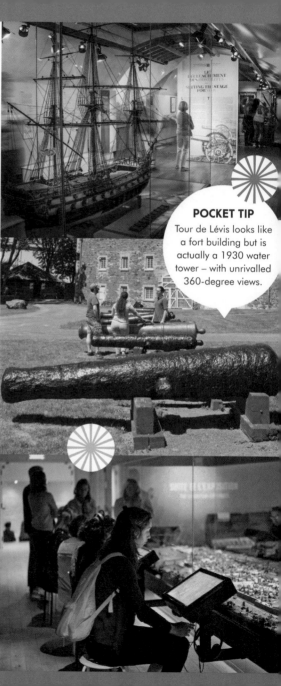

POCKET TIP
Tour de Lévis looks like
a fort building but is
actually a 1930 water
tower – with unrivalled
360-degree views.

18

2 LA GRANDE ROUE DE MONTRÉAL

362 Rue de la Commune Est,
Old Port
514 325 7888
www.lagranderouedemontreal.
com
Open daily 10am–11pm
[MAP p. 165 E2]

You know how you get up
to an observation deck and
think, 'OK, I've seen the view,
now what'? The best thing
about the 'Great Wheel' is
that the 360-degree panorama
keeps changing as the 42
gondolas go round and round,
peaking at 60 metres (about
200 feet) above ground – that's
20 storeys up. You get an eyeful
of everything worth seeing in
Montréal. On one side is the
massive Saint Lawrence River,
and some little mountains
beyond (visibility is up to
28 kilometres, or 17 miles, on
clear days). On the other
is Old Montréal's heritage
charm, downtown's towers
and Mont Royal (see p. 82).
At night, darkness is scattered
with a million lights, from the
illuminated cross atop Mont
Royal to the Jacques Cartier
Bridge's high-tech display.
Rides last about 20 minutes
through numerous rotations
in climate-controlled gondolas
made of huge amounts of
glass (number 42 even has
a glass floor).

3 BOTA BOTA

Corner Rue McGill and Rue de
la Commune Est, Old Port
514 284 0333
www.botabota.ca
Open daily 9am–11pm
(summer); other seasonal
hours vary
[MAP p. 167 D2]

Québecers love Nordic-style
spas: indoor-outdoor complexes
where steam and water, from
icy to hot, is the recipe for
rejuvenation. Most are out of
town amid forested landscapes,
but Bota Bota is in the middle
of Montréal with panoramic
views of the Saint Lawrence
River and Old Montréal. The
primo location is thanks to its
unusual structure: a 1950s ferry
permanently docked in the Old
Port. Admire the Scandi-chic
makeover as you sweat it out
in the saunas (four dry, two
steamy), plunge into cold baths
and float like a happy boiled
dumpling before completing
the circuit on the adjacent
leafy quay. Try its pools heated
to various temperatures, get
a natural shoulder massage
under the waterfall, then
snooze in a hammock or
deckchair. In freezing winter,
don't underestimate the joy
of slipping into warm water.
There are various treatments,
an on-board restaurant for
healthy salads and naughty
brownies, and discounted
access on Monday to
Thursday mornings.

4 LA RONDE

22 Chemin Macdonald, Parc
Jean-Drapeau
514 397 2000
www.sixflags.com/larondeen
Open late May to late Oct,
varying hours
[MAP p. 169 B2]

Do you love amusement parks
but hate how they are often
miles from anywhere? Good
news: La Ronde is one Métro
station from downtown – part
of the epic view from this park's
high-flying rides. Yes, there
are family rides, from the retro
elevated monorail built for
the '67 Expo, to the dodgems
(known poetically as autos
tamponneuses in French). But
if you're like me, amusement
parks are about rides that send
your stomach through your
feet, so don't miss Goliath –
this extreme rollercoaster
maxes out at 53-metres-high
(178 feet) and 110 kilometres
(68 miles) per hour. My other
irresistibles are Ednör, which
puts you into 360-degree spirals
and possibly a water jet, and
the bone-rattling Monstre, the
world's tallest two-track wooden
rollercoaster. Fuel up at the
many restaurants and snack
stands, including **Queues de
Castor** (*see* p. 25). Lines can be
painful during weekends and
school holidays, and there's no
avoiding big entry fees but save
online or buy a season pass.

5 TYROLIENNE MTL ZIPLINE

363 Rue de la Commune Est,
Hangar 16, Old Port
514 947 5463
www.mtlzipline.com
Open daily 11am–9pm
(summer); other seasonal hours
vary
[MAP p.165 E2]

You've arrived at Canada's first urban zipline: step into the harness, whack on a helmet and strap phone to wrist with the transparent pouch provided. Staff can help attach GoPros to helmets too, because there's a very likeable social media video and photo op ahead – after you've climbed the stairs to the top of the 24-metre-high (80 foot) tower. From there it's plain sailing as you zoom high above the Old Port's Bonsecours Basin, where others might be noodling around in peddle boats. Remember to take in the view, because the 360-metre-long (1180 feet) flight will be over before you know it. Two ziplines run parallel, so try a tandem jump with a friend. There's also Canada's first urban free-fall experience, which costs the same as the zipline, or save with a combo ticket.

POCKET TIP
Neighbouring Voiles en Voiles is an aerial adventure course through mock 18th-century ships – check it out if travelling with kids.

6 ſAUTE MOUTONſ JET BOATING

Departs from Clock Tower Pier,
Old Port
514 284 9607
www.jetboatingmontreal.com
Open daily May–Oct,
departures vary.
[MAP p. 165 F2]

Saute moutons means jumping
sheep. It sounds sleepy, but
actually refers to the white
water leaping along the
Lachine Rapids, where this
jet-boating business has
thrilled urban adventurers
since 1983. Its vessels are
custom-built for these rapids,
rated between four and five on
the International Scale of River
Difficulty, which goes up to
six – or virtually impassable,
at least for unpowered craft.
Nothing can prepare you for
that first wave crashing over
the open deck: unless you're
wearing supplied waterproofs
(no need on warm days),
you're instantly drenched
to your underwear. The water's
weight feels immense when
it explodes over you, then
swirls around your legs and
drains away. Again and again,
plunging up and down the
rapids on a rollercoaster ride
gone off the rails, each time
more wet and wild. Finally,
after some 360-degree spins,
there's a high-powered bolt
back to port.

POCKET TIP

Adrenaline junkies,
step right up to the
Décalade, a face-
first abseil, or rappel,
down the Old Port's
conveyor tower.

7 QUEUES DE CASTOR

123 Rue de la Commune Est,
Old Port
Open Mon–Thurs 12pm–11pm,
Fri–Sun 12pm–12am
www.beavertails.com
[MAP p. 165 D3]

Beaver tails are a bit doughy, but usually crisp and served with various sweet toppings. Don't worry, Canadians don't eat real beaver tails: it's what they call long, flat doughnuts, hand-stretched into a beaver-tail shape. Except in French-speaking parts like Montréal where they're queues de castor. Yummy in either language, beaver tails were born across the provincial border in Ontario in 1978 and are especially good on chilly days when the freshly fried warmth seeps into your hands. I love the classic Killaloe Sunrise: sugar, cinnamon and a lemon wedge. A local friend is crazy for the apple cinnamon with caramel, while kids go for heavy-hitting combos like chocolate, peanut butter and Reese's Pieces. Forget the maple option: it's just 'maple-flavoured' spread – an abomination here in the province that produces most of the world's maple syrup.

POCKET TIP

There's another Queues de Castor shop across the street in the Old Port's food court, and seasonally at La Ronde (see p. 22) amusement park.

25

8 TERRASSE SUR L'AUBERGE

6th floor, Rue 97 de la
Commune Est, Old Port
514 876 0081
www.terrassesurlauberge.com
Open Mon–Thurs 2–11pm,
Fri–Sun 12pm–11pm May–Sept
[MAP p. 185 B2]

From this rooftop terrasse, laid out before you is the Saint Lawrence River, the heritage buildings along Rue de la Commune, including Marché Bonsecours' silver dome, the Old Port's clock tower and Jacques Cartier Bridge. Then there's Île Sainte Hélène's big geodesic dome, and summer's weeks-long international fireworks competition. Yes, it's a VIP-worthy panorama, yet the menu, from shrimp cocktails to legit cocktails, is reasonably priced. There's a hefty cover charge on fireworks nights though, so check the International des Feux competition's schedule. Prices for whole bottles of spirits might also make you pause – then realise it's a fair deal when sharing with a few buddies. The one serious hurdle is Montréal's climate, which means Terrasse sur l'Auberge is only open May to September. The rest of the year, check out L'Auberge du Vieux-Port's other, street-level place to eat and drink, **Taverne Gaspar**.

POCKET TIP

The three-level Terrasses Bonsecours is right beside the river and has postcard-worthy views of the city skyline – especially at sunset.

DOWNTOWN

Commerce and culture thrive side by side in Montréal's downtown, or centre-ville. The main east-west axis, Sainte Catherine Street, hums with human activity. It's one of Canada's major shopping destinations, with desirable international brands' stores, local favourites and department stores, including the modern iteration of the world's oldest company: a fur-trading enterprise established in 1670 called the Hudson's Bay Company. A sure sign that Montréal is Canada's cultural capital is the one-square-kilometre zone designated the Quartier des Spectacles. Nothing to do with optometry, it means 'district of shows', and is packed with cultural venues and institutions, a massive outdoor performance space, playful projections and other public, often interactive, art. This is a UNESCO City of Design after all. If you want sport, visit the Bell Centre (*see p. 34*) (see p. 34) to watch some ice hockey – almost the only game in town, and an obsession for most.

By law there's nothing higher in Montréal than small but iconic Mont Royal, the up-close natural backdrop to downtown's concrete and glass. So, while it doesn't rate as far as big skyscrapers go, below street level it's a different story called the Underground City. Along 33 kilometres (21 miles) of downtown tunnels, hundreds of businesses, especially shops and eateries, plus numerous Métro stations, are linked to key ground-level destinations, from hotels to theatres. So it's possible to tick everything off without going outside – a heartwarming idea when it's wet or freezing.

Métro stations: Champ-de-Mars, Place d'Armes, Square-Victoria-OACI, Bonaventure, Lucien L'Allier, Peel, McGill, Place-des-Arts, Berri-UQAM

→ *Crescent Street mural celebrating late, great Montréaler Leonard Cohen*

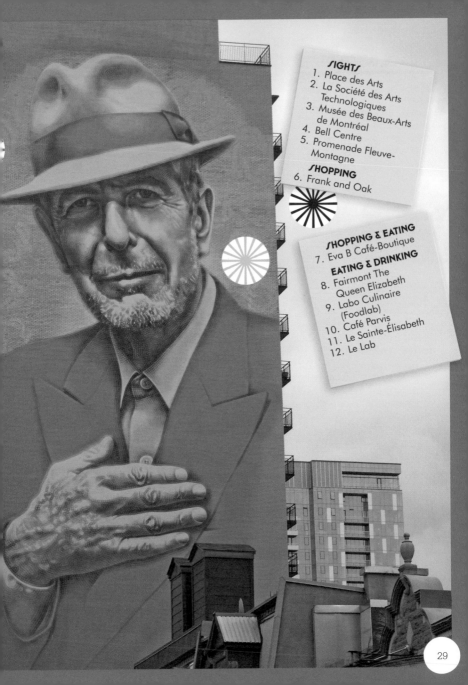

SIGHTS
1. Place des Arts
2. La Société des Arts Technologiques
3. Musée des Beaux-Arts de Montréal
4. Bell Centre
5. Promenade Fleuve-Montagne

SHOPPING
6. Frank and Oak

SHOPPING & EATING
7. Eva B Café-Boutique

EATING & DRINKING
8. Fairmont The Queen Elizabeth
9. Labo Culinaire (Foodlab)
10. Café Parvis
11. Le Sainte-Élisabeth
12. Le Lab

1 PLACE DEſ ARTſ

175 Rue Sainte-Catherine Ouest
514 842 2112
www.placedesarts.com
Box office open Mon–Sat
12pm–6pm (later during
performances), Sun check
performance schedule.
[MAP p. 161 F1, 164 A2]

At the heart of Montréal's arts district, Quartier des Spectacles, is Place des Arts, a complex of performance venues from the 1960s to the 2011 concert hall and Canada's first public gallery for contemporary art, the **MAC**. If you've seen the likes of Amy Schumer and Dave Chappelle on TV at 'Just for Laughs', the world's biggest comedy festival, it happened here, in the 3000-seat Salle Wilfrid-Pelletier. Place des Arts also hosts the world's biggest jazz festival's headliners, Opéra de Montréal and Les Grands Ballets Canadiens. The other major resident company is the Orchestre Symphonique de Montréal. Performances from anywhere and of almost any size land in its various venues through the year, including during the intense winters, when direct indoor access to underground parking and the Métro station is very welcome. The coat-check service even has tubs for shoes, so you can switch from snow boots to dainty heels.

2 LA SOCIÉTÉ DES ARTS TECHNOLOGIQUES

1201 Blvd Saint-Laurent
514 844 2033
www.sat.qc.ca
Box office opens two hours
before performances.
[MAP p. 164 B2]

Better known as SAT, this institution in the Quartier des Spectacles is dedicated to digital culture: design, video art, motion graphics, virtual reality and music. A lot of the building is for research, training and artist development, but its crowning glory, the Satosphère, is where cutting-edge digital art finds its audience. This 13-metre-high, 18-metre-wide (43 by 59 foot) dome forms a planetarium-style 360-degree projection screen where immersive experiences wow folks sprawled on the floor. Geek out with the digital music-and-video presentations, which can be mind-blowing, and look out for the summer dance parties under the dome. SAT's other public areas host events like one of the best grassroots design markets in this UNESCO City of Design, the annual Souk@SAT. The restaurant, **Labo Culinaire** (aka Foodlab, *see* p. 40) is the ideal place for refreshment pre- and post-show, or any time.

3 MUSÉE DE/ BEAUX-ART/ DE MONTRÉAL

1380 Rue Sherbrooke Ouest
514 285 2000
www.mbam.qc.ca
Open Tues–Sun 9am–5pm
(Wed until 9pm for major
exhibitions)
[MAP p. 161 D3]

On my first visit to the Montréal Museum of Fine Arts, I missed the entire international collection. Next time, I found those big guns like El Greco and Monet using a map of Montréal's largest museum, spread over several buildings connected by tunnels. Yet another wing (with panoramic views) was added in 2016. Find the Canadian collection in Bourgie Pavilion, a 19th-century church with Tiffany & Co stained-glass windows. Don't miss the Inuit artists' otherworldly Arctic sculptures; early 20th-century landscapes by Toronto's pioneering Group of Seven; and Montréal peers the Beaver Hall Group's portraits and streetscapes. Plus the decorative art and design collection and sculpture garden. The permanent collection is free for under-31s, and everyone on the first Sunday of the month. Major temporary exhibitions are half price on Wednesday evenings – but expect crowds.

4 BELL CENTRE

1909 Ave des Canadiens
de Montréal
855 310 2525
www.centrebell.ca
Open according to event
schedule.
[MAP p. 161 F3]

So you've heard that Canadians love hockey – ice hockey of course, and nowhere is this more true than Montréal. Visiting this stadium is a pilgrimage for sports lovers, even those who aren't fans of the legendary Montréal Canadiens, who call the Bell Centre home. Not sporty? Go on, catching a game will take you a long way towards understanding this city. Montréal's National Hockey League team, also known as the Habs (short for 'les habitants', the 17th-century French migrants), play about 50 games here each year – more if they're in the play-offs. They always sell out, so get in early – and expect to sit up in the nosebleeds if you're not cashed up. Otherwise, there are several hour-long guided tours in English on non-event days. It's all about the red, white and blue, from the lounge for former players and the surprisingly lounge-like locker room to corporate boxes and press gallery. Tours end in the gift shop where serious Montréal souvenirs like Habs jerseys and player bobble-heads beckon.

POCKET TIP
Get among the hockey memorabilia at the Forum, home to the Habs until 1996 and now an edge-of-downtown shopping entertainment complex.

5 PROMENADE FLEUVE-MONTAGNE

www.ville.montreal.qc.ca/
fleuve-montagne
Open daily 24-hours
[MAP p. 161 D2, 165 D4, 166 C1]

A pedestrian route created for Montréal's 375th anniversary in 2017, the 'river-mountain walk' is an enjoyable way to sample the city's history, public art and architecture. Most of the 3.8 kilometre (four mile) promenade is downtown, though it begins by the Saint Lawrence River in Old Montréal. I prefer the opposite direction, starting at the foot of Mont Royal and taking in the elevated views while ambling downhill. The project essentially enhanced what was already there, including transforming a street through leafy McGill College into a pedestrian space. Route highlights include Raymond Mason's huge 1986 sculpture, *The Illuminated Crowd*, which looks like a curious bunch of cartoonish people made of butter; the Art Deco tower built in 1929 as the Bell Telephone Company's headquarters; and an actual Paris Métro entrance, gifted to Montréal when the subway opened here in 1967. The promenade map reveals 100-plus points of interest, and is available from tourist info centres, major hotels or the website (there's no app).

POCKET TIP

The McCord Museum, a built-heritage stop near the promenade's mountain end, is worth visiting for more in-depth Montréal social history.

6 FRANK AND OAK

1420 and 1432 Rue Stanley
514 228 3761
www.frankandoak.com
Open Mon–Wed 10am–7pm,
Thurs–Fri 10am–9pm, Sat
10am–6pm, Sun 11am–5pm
[MAP p. 161 E2]

Champions of locally designed fashion, Frank and Oak is a top option both for fashionistas and those who prefer classics. They've nailed quality, affordable basics for guys and girls plus on-trend pieces, and are big on ethical and sustainable practises like water-efficient denim. This 2012 online menswear start-up was shipping 12,000 orders per month within a year, then opened stores across Canada and expanded into womenswear. In 2018, their downtown flagship store went all-man with three floors of classics, like shirts, blazers, jeans and sweaters, plus a barbershop. Womenswear moved to a dedicated store next door, offering smart looks that take you from airport to art gallery, from office to dinner, including dresses, coats and blouses. This femme zone also has a section dedicated to Montréal creatives working outside fashion, so you can pick up other distinctive made-in-Montréal souvenirs, like notebooks and natural skincare.

POCKET TIP
Other destinations for locally designed fashion include Onze, Evelyn, Éditions de Robes and Boutique Unicorn.

7 EVA B CAFÉ-BOUTIQUE

2015 Blvd Saint-Laurent
514 849 8246
www.eva-b.ca
Open Mon–Sat 11am–7pm,
Sun 12pm–6pm
[MAP p.161 F1, 162 A4]

Hours of rewarding rummaging and browsing awaits in this sprawling second-hand store. For decades its two floors have reeled in students, artists and thrifty shoppers seeking cheap, distinctive clothes and accessories in particular, as well as everything from books to furniture. You won't discover high-end designer vintage, and Eva B's artistically organised chaos may be off-putting to minimalists, but for everyone else it's a creative, eclectic place made for lingering. That mindset is helped along by free treats like petite packets of homemade popcorn, the occasional inspiring vignette (usually including mannequin parts) and signs with bon mots like 'Cinderella is proof that a new pair of shoes can change your life'. Quick bargains abound: maybe a classic black-and-red checked lumberjack shirt, futuristic 1970s earrings or weird plush toy. There's also an in-store cafe that extends from kitsch indoor dining nook to a pleasant outdoor deck. The menu, which includes samosas, soup and subs, makes beautiful reading for vegetarians.

POCKET TIP
Gentlemen! For a vintage look that's not pre-loved, go to Henri Henri, the place for dapper hats since 1932.

8 FAIRMONT THE QUEEN ELIZABETH

900 Blvd Réné Lévesque Ouest
514 861 3511
www.fairmont.com/queen-elizabeth-montreal
Open daily 24-hours
[MAP p. 161 F2]

Did you know John Lennon and Yoko Ono's 1969's 'bed-in for peace' happened here? The glory had faded when the Queen closed for renovations in 2016. She emerged transformed, a modernist-meets-contemporary designer destination, and not just for those who can afford to stay. It's now an art hotel in all but name, and most of the 123 artworks are in public areas, including three lithographs by Montréal's hottest 20th-century artist, Jean-Paul Riopelle, and the vintage stained-glass panels in the new **Marché Artisans**. This gourmet food hall has gifts, picnic treats and meals to go, and sleek counters for dining in on freshly prepared pleasures like charcuterie and crepes. Live it up on a budget at **Rosélys** restaurant with their 4–7pm happy-hour menu, or sip classy cocktails at the glam-rock-inspired **Nacarat** bar. If you *can* afford to stay, try the artfully transformed **Suite 1742**, where 'Give Peace a Chance' was written and recorded during the bed-in.

POCKET TIP
Have drinks with Warhol, Chagall and co at Old Montréal's LHotel, which is filled with modern and contemporary art.

9 LABO CULINAIRE (FOODLAB)

3rd floor, 1201 Blvd Saint-
Laurent
514 844 2033
www.sat.qc.ca/foodlab
Open Tues–Sat 5–10pm
[MAP p. 164 B1]

It's worth checking out La Société des Arts Technologiques (*see* p. 31) even when there's no event on, just because of the restaurant Labo Culinaire, aka Foodlab. It maintains the venue's creative attitude with artfully prepared seasonal, and often regional, ingredients. How about a mezze plate of naked oat salad, field pea hummus, herbed labneh, eggplant and cucumber? An all-Québec cheese platter or marinated trout with carraway sour cream, wild vegetables and wild rice? Alongside this affordable gastronomy is thoughtfully selected booze like the 'Montréal' cocktail made with local St. Laurent gin, and a long list of natural wines from around the world. Choose from the sleekly designed but welcoming indoor dining space or the warm-weather rooftop terrasse, where party lights and glowing city views conjure a little magic at night.

10 CAFÉ PARVIƧ

433 Rue Mayor
514 764 3589
www.cafeparvis.com
Open Mon–Wed 7am–11pm,
Thurs–Fri 7am–12am, Sat
10am–12am, Sun 10am–10pm
[MAP p. 161 F2]

Parvis: a medieval term for the
enclosed public area in front of
a church, based on the Latin
word for 'paradise'. Embodying
the word, this day–night
cafe is a secluded downtown
oasis tucked in a little street
opposite a Gothic Revival
church. The fare's slightly
posh yet affordable, and the
decor has an understated style
synonymous with interior
designer and co-owner
Zébulon Perron. Relax on mix
'n' match vintage wooden
furniture amid distressed paint
and early 20th-century marble
columns, as plants cascade
from horizontal planters above
and light streams through floor-
to-ceiling windows looking
onto the street. The menu
changes regularly, but there's
always several inventive salads
in three sizes that adapt from
solo lunches to shared sides.
Take a sophisticated coffee
break, or linger over pizzas
with toppings like goats
cheese, pear and lamb. Drinks
include well-crafted cocktails.

POCKET TIP
Furco, the associated
bar with a similar je
ne sais quoi, is next
door if you want to
kick on.

DOWNTOWN

11 LE SAINTE-ÉLISABETH

1412 Rue Sainte-Élisabeth
514 286 4302
www.ste-elisabeth.com
Open daily 3pm–3am
[MAP p. 162 C4]

The inconspicuous entrance
down a side street makes
what's behind it a real
surprise – especially the
awesome split-level terrasse
out the back of this self-
described 'pub Européen'.
A substantial outdoor space
filled with tables and chairs,
it's surrounded by red-brick
walls, covered in lush green
ivy during the warmer months.
Even when it's packed, it
has a secluded calm far
removed from downtown's
bustle. Add a few beers, and
ideally a few friends too, and
you've got yourself a classic
Montréal moment. Inside,
red-painted brick walls and
wooden furniture equal cosy
and convivial, especially when
the weather cools and you've
scored one of the leather
booths. There's a good if
unremarkable mix of imported
and local beers on tap and
a decent whisky selection
too, but don't come here for
the food. The small menu
of typical pub snacks, like
poutine, is from a nearby diner,
so it's delivered in take-out
packaging – sometimes after a
long wait.

12 LE LAB

279 Rue Sainte-Catherine Est
514 903 6522
www.barlelab.com
Open Sun–Mon 3pm–1am,
Tues–Wed 11am–1am, Thurs–
Fri 11am–3am, Sat 3pm–3am
[MAP p. 162 C4]

When bartender Fabien
Maillard moved to Montréal,
he found nothing like the
sophisticated cocktail scene
he knew in Paris. So the
Frenchman opened the original
Le Lab on the Plateau in 2008,
revolutionising the city's bar
culture with his crafty, seasonal
cocktails and training up part-
timers into professionals. Some
have gone on to launch their
own cool bars, but Le Lab, now
downtown, is still my Montréal
gold standard. You don't need
a gold credit card to enjoy top
tipples at this relaxed, slightly
nostalgic establishment.
Cocktails are available for half
price between 5 and 8pm and
are equal to anything else on
the long, ever-evolving menu,
lovingly styled with vintage
illustrations. Also lock eyes
on the board of nicely priced
monthly specials and the food
menu that ranges from classy
bar snacks like charcuterie
and cheeses to a handful of
substantial lunchtime offerings,
including smoked bacon
burgers. Raise a glass to the
past and say santé (cheers!)
to innovation.

PLATEAU-MONT-ROYAL

Only a few decades ago, this neighbourhood was the working class setting for hard-scrabble novels by Montréal's most acclaimed 20th-century writers, Mordecai Richler and Michel Tremblay. Now it's where the cool kids hang out. Among the classic triplexes with exterior stairs, the bike lanes, alleys, street art and parks, you'll find the biggest concentration of Montréal's best shops, bars, restos and cafes.

Most of the neighbourhood is known as The Plateau to locals, and has been gentrified. This means rising rents, ruelles vertes ('green' laneways), and awesome ways to blow your vacation budget. A stroll along the main drags of Rue Saint-Denis and Avenue Mont-Royal will soon reveal your heart's desire (or at least your stomach's). Boulevard Saint-Laurent, also known as The Main, used to be the dividing line between Montréal's English- and French-speaking communities. West of here is Mile End, where gentrification is about a decade behind The Plateau, and it's more multicultural too. There's a large Jewish population, who have made Mile End the epicentre for two out of three Montréal fast-food staples: bagels and smoked-meat sandwiches (more on poutine shortly!).

Métro stations: Sherbrooke, Mont-Royal and Laurier

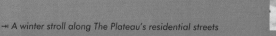
→ A winter stroll along The Plateau's residential streets

SIGHTS
1. Official Montréal Mural Tour

SHOPPING
2. Librairie Drawn and Quarterly
3. Aux 33 Tours
4. Tresnormale

EATING & DRINKING
5. La Banquise
6. St-Viateur Bagel
7. Sushi Momo
8. Cardinal Tea Room
9. Dieu du Ciel!

1 OFFICIAL MONTRÉAL MURAL TOUR

Start 3523 Blvd Saint-Laurent
www.spadeandpalacio.com
Tours Sat–Sun 10am–12pm
[MAP p.168 C4]

Street art is by definition
unsanctioned, but it's so
accepted, even officially
supported here that it's
blurring into public art.
Murals brighten and intrigue
the city – spectacularly so
along Mile End's stretch of
Boulevard Saint-Laurent,
where Spade & Palacio runs
the Official Montréal Mural
Tour. Official because they do
it in association with **Mural
Festival**, which began in 2013
and keeps getting bigger –
check it out if you're here in
June. Most murals created by
local and international artists
during this live street-art fair
meets block party are painted
over with new works during
the next festival, but some
become permanent – like
2017's nine-storey portrait
of Montréal legend Leonard
Cohen. The two-hour guided
walks take in major festival
murals, the ever-changing
street art, and rarely touched
pieces by Scaner, one of the
city's graffiti kings who died
in 2017. So about 25 works
in all. Like what you see?
The starting point, **Station
16 Gallery** specialises in
street art.

POCKET TIP
There's another massive
Leonard Cohen mural
downtown, on Crescent
Street (see p.29).
Some have mistaken
it for fellow late great,
Anthony Bourdain.

2 LIBRAIRIE DRAWN AND QUARTERLY

211 Rue Bernard Ouest,
Mile End
514 279 2224
www.drawnandquarterly.com
Open daily 10am–8pm
[MAP p. 170 C2]

No, not a library, but a bookstore – which is librairie in French. And what a bookstore this is, not because it's huge, but because it's got the coolest books and literary events in town. That includes a neat range of comics and graphic novels out of left field, because Drawn and Quarterly is first and foremost a publisher of some of the world's best cartoonists, like Daniel Clowes, Chris Ware and Kate Beaton. The book to buy here is *Drawn and Quarterly: Twenty-five Years of Contemporary Cartooning, Comics, and Graphic Novels*, a hefty, 776-page celebration of the publisher's output since cranking out a humble magazine in 1989. There's plenty more to choose from though, mostly in English but also French, from edgy novels and kids reads to beautiful art books and tomes revealing Montréal's secrets and oddities. You can also pick up a copy of the *Montréal Review of Books*, a free newspaper about Québec's books and writers. Staff are knowledgeable and passionate, and each curate a section of the store.

3 AUX 33 TOURƧ

1373 Ave Mont-Royal Est,
The Plateau
514 524 7397
www.aux33tours.com
Open Mon–Wed 10am–7pm,
Thurs–Fri 10am–9pm, Sat–Sun
10am–6pm
[MAP p. 168 B1]

Aux 33 Tours means 'at 33 RPM', the speed 12-inch records are played. If that gives you goosebumps, don't miss this store, which specialises in vinyl from far and wide. Stacks of it, all lovingly curated by staff obsessed with music and the sensory pleasures of good old-fashioned records. Everything that's new on wax is almost certainly here, whether it's a Prince reissue or the latest from locals Arcade Fire, limited editions or what audiophiles crave: Japanese pressings (anyone here will tell you that the sound quality, even the packaging, is the business). There's a huge range of used records too, from classical and country, to bebop and hip hop, each labelled with carefully considered info including the condition of the vinyl and sleeve. They also stock hardware such as turntables, amps and needles, as well as pre-loved CDs and cassettes. Montréal's biggest and best independent music store got bigger and better in 2018 when it expanded next door.

4 TRE∫NORMALE

207 Ave Fairmount Ouest,
Mile End
514 836 9702
www.tresnormale.com
Open Mon–Wed & Sat–Sun
11.30am–6pm, Thurs–Fri
11.30am–8pm
[MAP p. 171 E3]

The shop's motto is 'T-shirts for normal people'. Sure, prices are aimed at normal folks, but these threads are genuinely special. The main attraction is the range of Montréal designs: mono- and duo-chrome renderings of everyday urban scenes, like the Fairmount bagel shop down the street, a Métro platform or the exterior of a triplex, those ubiquitous low-rise apartment blocks of the inner-city. These tees, made for men, women and kids, plus a handful of tote bags, are souvenirs with street cred. They are designed and silk-screened in-store by Jörn, who hails from Berlin but wears his Montréal heart on his sleeve. 'I think an outsider has a better eye for what makes a city peculiar,' he says. While you're here, check out the philosopher, writer and poet designs. Their wit is obscurely intellectual (like the portrait of Albert Camus emblazoned with 'Stranger Danger'). Or keep it simple with one of Jörn's whimsical designs – perhaps the shop's logo of a cartoonish figure peering into a dark doorway.

femmes . women

POCKET TIP
Discover more locally designed Montréal souvenirs nearby at Artpop, 129 Ave Mont-Royal Est.

5 LA BANQUISE

994 Rue Rachel Est, The Plateau
514 525 2415
www.labanquise.com
Open daily 24-hours
[MAP p. 168 B1]

Summer and winter, day or
night, every time I come by
this family-run fast-food joint
there's a line out the door. It's
popular, but I didn't realise just
how popular, and how famous,
until I saw some tourists – all
the way from Asia – pile out
of a taxi with their luggage
and join the queue. What's
the big deal? The hot mess of
fries, cheese curds and gravy
known as poutine, which
may be the world's ugliest,
most satisfying comfort food.
This cheap, quintessential
Montréal dish, rumoured to
have been invented in nearby
Drummondville during the
1950s, is all over town, but La
Banquise has consistently been
the local go-to for decades.
They take the carb-elicious
favourite beyond its classic
three ingredients with 30-plus
variations, including Mexican,
smoked meat and vegan.
There are other options, like
hot dogs and burgers, but this
is the poutine epicentre of the
universe, so why would you?
The best times for immediate
seats are the wee small hours
and weekdays either side
of lunch.

6 ST-VIATEUR BAGEL

263 Ave Saint-Viateur Ouest,
Mile End
514 276 8044
www.stviateurbagel.com
Open daily 24-hours
[MAP p. 171 D3]

POCKET TIP

Fairmount Bagel is nearby at 74 Ave Fairmount Ouest. For Montréal's other Jewish treat, smoked-meat sandwiches, try Schwartz's or Wilensky's.

It's not a question of whether you eat bagels in Montréal, it's whether you buy them from Fairmount or St-Viateur. So this book makes my allegiance clear, but the truth is any decent Montréal bagelry is conjuring better golden rings of joy than anywhere else in the world. That includes NYC, because in Montréal they're less dense and the exterior's more crisp. There's also the faintest hint of sweetness, because honey is traditionally added to the water that Montréal bagels are boiled in. The original St-Viateur was opened in 1957 by a Polish refugee in the heart of the city's Jewish neighbourhood. It's still going strong, with several more outlets besides. St-Viateur's bagels are so good they're shipped across Canada and to the US as well. Watch bagels being baked in the wood-fired oven while a few, still warm and soft, are scooped into a paper bag for you. Breathe in that deeply satisfying scent of comfort. Hot tip: the sesame bagels are best, especially with a schmear of cream cheese.

51

7 SUSHI MOMO

3609 Rue Saint-Denis,
The Plateau
514 825 6363
www.sushimomo.ca
Open Wed–Thurs & Sun
3–10pm, Fri–Sat 3–10.30pm
[MAP p. 162 A2, 168 C3]

Sushi Momo blows my mind
every time with its all-vegan,
all-delicious menu. It began in
2014 as a tiny resto that soon
went 100% veg, then twice
relocated to bigger, fancier digs
nearby. The menu is dominated
by numerous maki sushi,
each a distinctly different
morsel of flavours, textures
and artful presentation. There
are obvious ingredients, like
avocado, cucumber and tofu,
but then there's pan-fried
jackfruit, yuzu emulsion and
mock shrimp tempura (there's
surprisingly little faux flesh
for such a long and diverse
vegan menu). Everything is
presented with a Japanese
eye for design, so a burst of
golden mango might nestle
beside a garnish of toasted rice
crispies and a swirl of long, fine
beetroot strands. Set menus,
including for solo diners, are
a good deal and bypass the
selection crisis with a generous
mix of sushi. There are other
dishes, such as poutine with
exotic mushrooms and teriyaki
miso, and plenty of gluten-free
options. It's often packed.

POCKET TIP

Feeling meaty and cashed
up? Au Pied de Cochon,
one of Montréal's most
revered restaurants,
specialises in carnivorous
Québecois fare.

8 CARDINAL TEA ROOM

5326 Blvd Saint-Laurent,
Mile End
514 903 2877
www.thecardinaltea.com
Open Thurs–Sun 11am–7pm
[MAP p. 171 E2]

When this upstairs space opened in 2013, Montréal got its afternoon-tea groove back. Co-owner Murad Meshgini says it was important to 'reintroduce this concept to young people'. It's not just for women, either. 'Nothing makes me happier than seeing a group of men huddled over tea and scones,' he adds. So there are pretty vintage china cups and saucers galore, but the decor favours old military and hunting prints, books, trophies and wooden tennis racquets reminiscent of venerable English gentlemen's clubs. There's also a swanky chandelier and baby grand piano, which gets tickled on weekends, but it's more casual than smart, with wooden chairs and comfy couches. Scones are fat, fluffy, blueberry-dotted beauties, served with various leaf teas, including delicate lavender Earl Grey, in cute red teapots, and the menu's must-have sandwich is creamy egg with fresh cress. Cardinal is equally ideal for quiet solo pauses and special get-togethers.

POCKET TIP
For seriously fancy afternoon tea, head to downtown's grand and historic Ritz-Carlton hotel.

9 DIEU DU CIEL!

29 Ave Laurier Ouest, Mile End
514 490 9555
www.dieuduciel.com
Open daily 11.30am–3am
[MAP p. 171 F3]

It roughly translates as 'God above!', but there's no need to thank a higher power for the beer at this brewpub, or microbrasserie. Just the guys who opened it in 1998 and continue to produce some of the best brews in a region renowned for craft beer. About 20 on tap are listed on the blackboard each day. They shift with the seasons, but it's always a diverse, mouth-watering mix. In summer, I love the Blanche du Paradis, a Belgian-style wheat beer that's light and citrusy and ideally enjoyed on the terrasse out front – if you can score a seat. In winter, cosy up inside among the well-worn wood and red-painted walls, perhaps with an Aphrodisiaque dark chocolate and vanilla stout. Whether it's rauchbier, IPA or a hibiscus-flower beer, it's good stuff served in the right style of glass. The board can be French-heavy, so if in doubt chat with the (naturally bilingual) staff or find inspiration in the bar's tap art. Each Dieu du Ciel! brew has its own original artwork, which you'll also see on their bottles around town. Bonus! Beer-friendly pub food is always available until late.

LITTLE ITALY

Maybe you've come to Montréal for a French experience, but spend some time in this neighbourhood where the city's joie de vivre gets an Italian spin. Since the 19th century, Italian migrants have gathered here in La Petite-Italie, but the main wave came after World War Two. There are now a quarter-million people with Italian ancestry living in Montréal (the second largest population in Canada), and chances are they have lived in this precinct, or have parents or grandparents who did. Pizza and pasta are everywhere, there are churches inspired by the mother country, and amici (friends) gather at coffee shops or play bocce in Parc Dante (named for the medieval Italian poet who's honoured with a statue there).

Italian flags flutter red, white and green, especially during August's Italian Week, and in May when the Grand Prix adds more colour and movement with chequered flags and fast cars. It's not all cannoli and lambrusco though. As migrants from the big boot began moving out in the late 20th century, other cultures moved in, as well as students and entrepreneurs, creating a vibrant multicultural vibe. That's added more bars, restos and shops to the mix, and more reasons to eat and drink your way around Little Italy.

Métro stations: Rosemont, Jean-Talon, De Castelnau, Parc

➥ A classic Montréal dépanneur (corner store), in Little Italy

/HOPPING
1. Alambika
2. Tah-Dah!

/HOPPING & EATING
3. Jean Talon Market

EATING & DRINKING
4. Caffè Italia
5. Trou de Beigne
6. La Brume dans mes Lunettes
7. Le Pourvoyeur
8. Pizzeria Napoletana
9. Impasto

1 ALAMBIKA

6484 Blvd Saint-Laurent
514 400 9212
www.alambika.ca
Open Mon–Fri 11am–7pm,
Sat–Sun 11am–5pm
[MAP p. 172 C4]

Montréal's craft cocktail scene has come a long way in a short time, in no small part thanks to this cocktail supply store. Opening in Outremont in 2012, then relocating to Little Italy six years later, Alambika is an Aladdin's cave for lovers of fine beverages. The glorious absinthe fountain might be a bit too pricey or specialised for the average shopper, but there are plenty of affordable, luggage-sized treasures that will really up your at-home cocktail game. What the mixologist in you really wants are those wicked tiki mugs or a couple of bitters from Alambika's bewildering selection. They've got shakers and jiggers, shiny metal julep cups and crystal highball glasses, muddlers and ice crushers. They've even got the smoking gun – the bartender's kind, should you be so serious about making cocktails that you want to serve 'em up in a puff of smoke. The knowledgeable staff can help you decide between a copper or stainless steel strainer, and the spruce or Spanish bitters.

2 TAH-DAH!

156 Rue Jean-Talon Est
514 271 1313
www.tah-dah.ca
Open Mon–Wed 11am–6pm,
Thurs–Fri 11am–7pm, Sat
10am–5pm, Sun 11am–5pm
[MAP p. 172 A2]

There's a constant flow of local creations in this UNESCO City of Design, and lots of them are gathered in this shop next to Jean Talon Market (*see* p. 62). Everything at Tah-dah! is designed, if not handmade, in the province of Québec, including T-shirts that celebrate this city with much more savoir faire than the usual souvenirs. (If you like the Tresnormale tees, find the full range at their shop; *see* p. 49). What about a cute and cuddly hand-knitted animal toy, or cushion covers with French expressions that are sophisticated even when lost in translation? Some distinctive jewellery by Coco Matcha, men's hair and skincare products by Groom or Makiko Hicher's ceramics? If you want a small low-priced keepsake, check out the little loose-change treasures like button badges and greeting cards. When you get home, they'll bring back fond memories of this creative store, which is as full of nice surprises as the name suggests.

61

3 JEAN TALON MARKET

7070 Ave Henri-Julien
514 937 7754
www.marchespublics-mtl.com
Open Mon–Wed & Sat 7am–
6pm, Thurs–Fri 7am–8pm,
Sunday 7am–5pm
[MAP p. 172 B2]

From late spring through summer, regional farmers sell their super-fresh fruits and vegetables at this huge market. Try their generous sample plates, from tomatoes to nectarines (don't be shy). My favourite stall is a truck full of the sweetest, juiciest corn, fresh-picked that day. After autumn's apples and chilli peppers disappear, there are lots of year-round options in the main building and around the market's perimeter. Try the oyster bar and crêperie, or get supplies for picnics and cooking – perhaps **Pastificio Sacchetto**'s fresh pasta or **Les Jardins Sauvages** foraged food, including mushrooms and young, coiled fern fronds called fiddleheads. For cookbooks go to **Librairie Gourmand**, and find 400-plus local producers' artisanal pleasures at **Marché des Saveurs du Québec**. From pâtés de caribou to all kinds of maple products and the province's other liquid gold, ice cider, this shop is the best place in town for le goût du Québec – the taste of Québec.

4 CAFFÈ ITALIA

6840 Blvd Saint-Laurent
514 495 0059
www.caffeitalia.ca
Open daily 6am–11pm
[MAP p. 172 B3]

'Ciao!' Again and again you hear this word exchanged between staff and customers like they're old friends. Often they are – plenty of regulars have been coming here for years, taking their favourite stool at the coffee bar. I'm an infrequent visitor, but that casual Italian charm gets me every time. Caffè Italia has hardly changed since it opened in 1956. Its lone renovation, in 2014, was about changing it as little as possible, so the bar is a replica and the terrazzo floor was merely buffed. There are two shiny espresso machines side-by-side, constantly in action; a few Italian products for sale, like Proraso shaving cream and classic stove-top coffee pots; a vintage clock advertising chinotto with an alluring picture of Sofia Lauren; and a fusball table out the back. It's like those old neighbourhood caffès in Italy, except that the minimalist menu's in French and includes peanut butter toast. Settle in for a sandwich and chinotto or coffee and cake. Pretend like you've always sat in that chair, then see if you don't say 'ciao!' on the way out.

brio
CHINOTT
THE SOFT DRINK OF ITAL

POCKET TIP
See vintage decor with OTT Italian style, including frescoes and Carrara marble, inside the Madonna della Difesa church.

5 TROU DE BEIGNE

156 Rue Saint-Zotique Est
514 701 3735
www.troudebeigne.com
Open Tues–Sun 9am–5pm
[MAP p. 172 B3]

How did a little beignet (doughnut) shop on a quiet street get 12K Instagram followers? By making an ever-evolving suite of sweets (sorry!) that are a feast for your eyes as much as your mouth. There are only two samples of the nine flavours displayed in a small glass cabinet in this simple space, overlooked by a massive yellow-eyed owl mural. But who needs more when these doughnuts are almost impossible to choose from? Maybe the summery sangria or lime-coconut? Or the S'More, which takes the messy campfire treat's ingredients and turns them into a beautiful anywhere, anytime indulgence. Can't decide? They are only a few dollars each, and even cheaper by the dozen – woohoo! (Pardon my owl.) The magic happens in the kitchen, where beignets are hand-rolled, fried and glazed each morning. I'm not going to claim they're healthy, but they are made with coconut oil rather than animal fats, and are free of corn syrup, preservatives, artificial colours and flavours. Can't get to the shop? Good news, couch potato – they deliver!

6 LA BRUME DANS MES LUNETTES

378 Rue Saint-Zotique Est
514 379 1178
www.labrumedansmeslunettes.
com
Open Mon–Fri 7.30am–7pm,
Sat–Sun 9am–7pm
[MAP p. 172 C2]

Need a laidback cafe to settle in with your laptop, good coffee and an affordable sandwich, soup or salad? Or are you looking for afternoon tea at a time that suits you? Either way, this is the place. The balancing act between casual and fancy is so adroitly done here that they even offer the sconewich: a scone (like an American biscuit) with yummy savoury fillings. Taking its name from a popular Québec song's lyrics, which translate as 'the mist in my glasses', this cafe is about comfort and contentment. Light streams through big windows onto functional furniture and two gracious armchairs. No matter how much coin or time you've got, there's a teatime service for you, right up to 'sa majesté la reine', the full sweet-and-savoury works on a three-tiered stand, including excellent scones, and tea in a silver pot – all delivered with a tongue-in-cheek 'God Save the Queen' jingle. Tea is always the best: from London's Fortnum & Mason, or Canada's Sloane.

POCKET TIP
Craving classic Italian cakes and pastries? Alati-Caserta have been making them right since 1968.

7 LE POURVOYEUR

184 Rue Jean-Talon Est
www.lepourvoyeur.com
Open Mon–Fri 11.30am–3am,
Sat–Sun 10am–3am
[MAP p. 172 A2]

Backing onto Jean Talon Market (*see* p. 62), this self-described gin pub that's relaxed by day and social at night is the best place to kick back after shopping. The food is gourmet-leaning pub grub inspired by the fresh produce that's steps away. From breakfast poutine loaded with egg and bacon to burgers with duck, brie and fig preserves and late-night snacks like mini corn dogs, the menu makes you want to stick around. Then there are the drinks, which satisfy all comers, but first and foremost this is a gin joint. There's a long, loving list of it, from familiar brands to obscure microdistilleries. Gin from England, no surprise there, but also countries you probably never knew made gin, like Italy and Colombia. Try local stuff from Montréal distilleries, such as Cirka, or two of my favourites from the province: Ungava, bright yellow because of its sub-arctic botanicals and Gin Neige, distilled by a boutique cider maker with a hint of apple. Gin this good is dandy for sipping, but Le Pourvoyeur also mix it up with top-notch tonic and craft quality cocktails.

8 PIZZERIA NAPOLETANA

189 Rue Dante
514 276 8226
www.napoletana.com
Open Mon–Thurs 11am–
10.30pm, Fri–Sat 11am–
11.30pm, Sun 12pm–10.30pm
[MAP p. 172 B3]

When Italian migrants arrived in the precinct after World War Two, this was one of the places where they came to get a taste of home. More of a bar with snack foods and pool tables when it opened in 1948, this landmark corner soon morphed into Montréal's first pizzeria. These days, countless locals make regular pilgrimages here, often firm in the opinion these are the best pizzas in town. In summer, especially weekend peak times, you should expect to wait for a table. Its popularity is partly about tradition – dining here with friends and family is almost as Montréal as eating poutine – and partly about the upbeat Mediterranean vibe. Then there's the pull of the pizzas: big, thin crusts with 41 topping combinations, from classic margherita to meaty salumeria. There are almost as many pasta dishes, plus favourite antipasto and Italian desserts, all nicely priced. You can bring your own wine, but payment is cash only – capiche?

POCKET TIP
There are hundreds of Montréal restaurants where you're welcome to bring your own wine (BYOB) or apportez votre vin.

9 IMPASTO

48 Rue Dante
514 508 6508
www.impastomtl.ca
Open Tue–Wed & Sat 5–11pm,
Thurs–Fri 11.30am–2pm &
5–11pm
[MAP p. 172 B3]

You're in Little Italy so of course you're going to eat Italian. Is it really Italian though? That's a resounding si certamente! (yes, of course!) at this resto, which is driven by tradition but also gently champions a fresh New World attitude. The Montréal-Italian guys behind Impasto know and love their stuff: Michele Forgione has cheffed at some of the city's best, and Stefano Faita, known for his cooking show and cookbooks, grew up at his parents' legendary kitchen-supply shop around the corner, **Quincaillerie Dante**. So no surprise the food's among the best in town for a mid-range price. It's fuelled by regional produce, and a lot of ingredients are made from scratch, including pasta and charcuterie. The wine list is 100% Italian imports. The smart-casual decor is by Zébulon Perron (see Café Parvis p. 41). There's usually a buzz of la dolce vita among the room's clean lines of tile, wood and leather, and in warm weather the big windows swing open onto a kerbside terrasse.

POCKET TIP
Want to take home some high-end kitchen equipment or just need something to ease accommodation cooking? Quincaillerie Dante has it.

69

LE/ QUARTIER/ DU CANAL

With its fortunes tied to the Lachine Canal's rise, fall and rehabilitation, this precinct is now emerging as Montréal's up-and-coming place to eat, drink, shop, play and live. Les Quartiers du Canal comprises three neighbourhoods that are increasingly home to young professionals but were once bywords for working-class: historically Irish Griffintown; Little Burgundy, formerly home to many people of African origin including jazz great Oscar Peterson; and French-speaking Saint-Henri. When the canal opened in 1825, ships could bypass the Lachine Rapids just upriver from Montréal, transforming it into a major port. Industry thrived along the canal, and fine public buildings and homes still standing today appeared amid factories and workers' hovels.

The industry has long gone but urban renewal programs, including the canal's reopening for pleasure boats in 2002, have seen condos rise so rapidly in Griffintown that little of its heritage remains. This boom has attracted designers to the area, to the point that in 2017 the local chamber of commerce declared a loose area covering several streets as an official design district. Walk, cycle or boat along the canal and explore all three neighbourhoods' post-industrial cool: warehouse and factory conversions, the iconic Five Roses flour neon sign and, from 2020, Griffintown's cultural complex made of old Métro trains.

Métro stations: Bonaventure, Lucien L'Allier, Georges Vanier, Lionel-Groulx, Place-Saint-Henri

→ Watching the day drift by on Atwater Quay's Canal Lounge

SIGHTS
1. Atwater Quay

SHOPPING
2. Vintage Frames Company
3. West Elm

SHOPPING & EATING
4. Atwater Market
5. Le Richmond

EATING & DRINKING
6. Rustique
7. Atwater Cocktail Club
8. McAuslan

4 CANAL LOUNGE

LES QUARTIERS DU CANAL

1 ATWATER QUAY

By the Lachine Canal's Ave
Atwater footbridge, Little
Burgundy
Open 24-hours
[MAP p. 173 C2]

Step across from **Atwater
Market** (*see* p. 75) and
discover one of the Lachine
Canal's nicest spots, where
you can boat, bike or relax
on a floating bar. Although
maybe not during winter,
because this area is bleaksville
when temperatures are down
and the wind's up. On the
boardwalk opposite the market,
Havre-aux-glaces opens
seasonally, serving sorbets
made from produce of the
moment such as blueberries
and nectarines, and ice-cream
flavours like burnt maple
caramel. A few steps further,
there's **Canal Lounge**, a
vintage canal-boat conversion
where on warm afternoons
you will absolutely want their
nautical-themed cocktails,
like Malibu Seabreeze. Across
the footbridge there's a shady
lawn, perfect for picnics from
the market. There's **H2O
Adventures** for renting
canoes, pedal boats, little
electric boats and kayaks; they
also do guided kayak tours
all the way to the Old Port.
Find two-wheel rentals at **Ma
Bicyclette**, right on the canal
bike path, which *Time* mag
rated as the world's third most
beautiful urban cycling route.

POCKET TIP
A Montréal skyline
highlight since the
1940s, the Five Roses
red neon sign is best
viewed canal-side
in Griffintown.

72

2 VINTAGE FRAME*J*
COMPANY

4411 Rue Notre-Dame Ouest,
Saint-Henri
438 381 4068
www.vintageframescompany.com
Open Tues–Wed & Sat
11am–5pm, Thurs–Fri
11am–8pm
[MAP p. 173 A3]

Vintage designer sunglass
and specs stores are popping
up all over, from New York to
Rome, and here in Montréal.
This black showroom with a
chandelier and shelves of old
bound books has hundreds
of rare frames to choose
from: lots displayed behind
glass, gleaming on prop
faux-gold bullion, and lots
more in the drawers below.
Balenciaga, Givenchy, Chanel,
Cartier, Hugo Boss, Ray-Ban,
Moschino et al, plus limited
edition vintage-inspired
newbies designed by the
man behind Vintage Frames
Company, Corey Shapiro.
You might see this larger-
than-life businessman here:
full, perfectly trimmed beard,
heavy jewellery including a
big gold chain, baseball cap
and, of course, dope glasses.
His customers include hip-hop
titans and movie stars who
are in the market for frames
with price tags in the tens of
thousands of dollars. For the
rest of us, there are options
under $200.

POCKET TIP
Get Shapiro's
gentleman gangsta
look with a haircut
or beard trim at his
barbershop just down
the street, Notorious.

3 WE/T ELM

995 Rue Wellington, Griffintown
514 861 2809
Open Mon–Wed 8am–7pm,
Thurs–Fri 8am–9pm, Sat
10am–7pm, Sun 10am–6pm
[MAP p. 166 B4]

I know, I know, West Elm is an
international chain that started
in Brooklyn, but this store has
a section called Local that
champions Montréal designers
and creators. Discover cute
tea towels and greeting cards,
crafty cocktail syrups and
bath salts, even an exclusive
selection of paintings and
drawings on paper by Montréal
artist Lysa Jordan. Then
there's the rest of this big,
light, bright store, filled with
sleek contemporary furniture
and more portable accessories
to covet – from linens to
ceramics – all displayed to
inspire the interior designer
in you to refine if not rethink
your lifestyle. There's also an
in-store cafe serving proper
coffee and sweet treats like
cookies and pastries, so you
can ponder these objects of
desire at leisure.

POCKET TIP

An elevated highway
recently made way for
Griffintown's mini-park
with two monumental
sculptures: Plensa's *Source*
and de Broin's stairs-to-
nowhere, *Dendrites*.

4 ATWATER MARKET

138 Ave Atwater, Little
Burgundy
514 937 7754
www.marchespublics-mtl.com
Open Mon–Wed 7am–6pm,
Thurs 7am–7pm, Fri 7am–8pm,
Sat–Sun 7am–5pm
[MAP p. 173 C2]

Atwater Market's big indoor–
outdoor experience happens
from May to October, but its
indoor heart is open year-
round. Summer means farm-
fresh juicy peaches, plums and
tomatoes, while autumn's a riot
of colourful pumpkins, gourds
and squash. Stroll through an
urban forest of Christmas trees
from late November, then in
spring frolic among thousands
of potted herbs and flowering
plants destined for gardens
and window boxes. During
the warmer months, food
stalls like **Satay Brothers** are
open, and it's a prime place
for gathering supplies for a
picnic on the Lachine Canal's
grassy bank. Indoors, **Le
Paradis du Fromage**'s three-
cheeses-for-$12 deal usually
solves my dilemma about
choosing between fromageries
(cheese shops), and **Première
Moisson**'s queue allows time
for deciding which breads
and pastries are the most
irresistible. **Les Douceurs
du Marché** is packed with
gourmet groceries, including
local treats like maple products
and artisinal condiments.

5 LE RICHMOND

377 Rue Richmond, Griffintown
514 508 8749
www.lerichmond.com
Open Mon–Sat 8am–10pm,
Sun 8am–6pm
[MAP p. 161 F4]

This food destination attracted a glamorous clientele from the get-go. It's a big old red-brick industrial space converted into twin vintage yet modern dining rooms with northern Italian tastes. **Le Restaurant** is a chandelier-lit space of lively conversation and music, cocktails, Champagne, and pricey dishes you can pimp up with extra foie gras or truffle. Then there's the more affordable bistro, **Le Marché Italien**, where casual dining leads to shopping for gourmet products and chic homewares. Its style is more restrained vintage-industrial, from chequered tile floor to marble bar. There's no hint of attitude from the staff, so lob up in practical travelling kit if needs must, from breakfast of duck confit benedict to dinnertime octopus carpaccio. Or pop in for the extensive Italian pantry's picnic and cooking supplies, like cheese, olives and pasta sauce. The kitchen-and-bath oriented products are even more elegantly presented, so you may leave with something stylish for your home too.

POCKET TIP
It may not look like Montréal's coolest resto, but Little Burgundy's budget-breaking Joe Beef requires bookings months in advance.

6 RUSTIQUE

4615 Rue Notre-Dame Ouest,
Saint-Henri
514 439 5970
www.rustiquepiekitchen.com
Open Mon–Fri 9am–6pm, Sat
9am–5pm, Sun 10am–5pm
[MAP p. 173 A3]

At this charming, classic
American-style bakery and
cafe, it's easy to tell what
time of year it is. The pies
change with the seasons, so
peaches, cherries and other
summer fruits make way for
autumn produce like apples
and pumpkin. 'It's always a
different seasonal play,' says
co-owner Jacqueline Berman.
'We're always keeping the
essence of the recipe the same,
then changing the emphasis
on flavour.' That means crusts
are handmade with real
butter, then filled with fruity
sweetness. Settle in with a
drink, from summery lemonade
to espresso and hot chocolate,
and a petite pie or two (slices,
scones and cookies are also on
offer). Then get a big pie to go
for a picnic or easy treat at your
accommodation. It's all artfully
displayed in this rustic yet
chic space with white-washed
wood panelling and gracious
text on blackboards. In 2017,
Rustique branched out next
door, where pies are filled with
savoury ingredients: cheese,
meat and vegetables, like kale
and mushrooms.

POCKET TIP
Sweet treats of the gourmet popsicle kind are nearby at Pops Art, an unexpected house-shop on a residential street (291 Beaudoin).

RUSTIQUE

breuvages

BR

TARTES 10' ..... 24.95 $
TARTELETTES 2' ..... 2.50 $

gâteaux
60$

INFORMEZ-VOUS
DE NOS
Services de
Traiteur

BARRES
biscuits
-SANDWICHS À LA

Breuvages
DU MOMENT

CAFÉ GLACÉ 3
CHAI LATTE GLACÉ 4
LIMONADE 3
THÉ GLACÉ 3
verger blanc + hibiscus

7 ATWATER COCKTAIL CLUB

512 Ave Atwater, Saint-Henri
438 387 4252
www.atwatercocktailclub.com
Open daily 5pm–3am
[MAP p. 173 B2]

This speakeasy-style bar takes a little bit of finding. See the First Nations chief painted on the door at the end of the little alley? Step inside through the heavy curtains to find a den with light so moody it takes several seconds to see the wall of bottles behind the marble bar, the low, reflective ceiling, wood-panelled walls and fuchsia banquettes. Yes, Atwater Cocktail Club is classy, and she's not just good looks. Cocktails, the stars of the long drinks list, are conjured from quality ingredients: fine spirits, of course, as well as ice chipped from one massive block, and fruits from the nearby market. Blackberries and blueberries are key to Smoke Show, the cocktail that lives up to its name as a glass dome filled with smoke is removed for the big reveal. Food also impresses, because it's from **Foiegwa**, the fancy-but-fun French diner next door. Poutine with truffled bechamel sauce? Oui, oui!

POCKET TIP
Party on at Griffintown's New Gas City, a huge music venue in an 1859 gasworks.

8 MCAUSLAN

5080 Rue Saint-Ambroise,
Saint-Henri
514 939 3060
www.mcauslan.com
Seasonal hours vary
[MAP p. 158 C4]

When husband-and-wife
team Peter McAuslan and
Ellen Bounsall established the
McAuslan brewery in 1988,
they produced just one beer:
St-Ambroise Pale Ale. It was
named for the street they set
up on, among the ruins of the
Lachine Canal's industrial
past, when they were the
only craft brewers in town.
Fast forward a few decades
and Montréal's beer scene's
'changed enormously,' says
McAuslan. Wildly popular on
warm weekends, yet always
laidback, the spring–through–
autumn terrasse overlooks one
of Saint-Henri's last untouched
industrial relics: rusting grain
silos, so picturesque beside the
green lawn and red umbrellas
on blue-sky days. Dog walkers,
cyclists, even kayakers mosey
in at the canal-side entrance
to savour a range from oatmeal
stout to grapefruit IPA, plus
bar food. Can't decide? Get
the six-beer tasting paddle. If
you're visiting outside terrasse
season, cosy up in the **Annexe**
bar. Regular behind-the-scenes
brewery tours include generous
tastings and are a bargain at $5
(all donated to charity).

ON & AROUND MONT ROYAL

At 233 metres (764 feet), it's more hill than mountain, but otherwise Mont Royal is a pretty big deal. This little peak that gave Montréal its name is downtown's natural backdrop, from green to autumn colour to winter white. Known locally as La Montagne (The Mountain), it's one of the city's largest green spaces. A sizeable chunk is Parc du Mont-Royal's semi-wilderness, designed by Frederick Law Olmsted of New York's Central Park fame. It's always popular, from cross-country skiing to Tam Tams (*see* p. 87), the warm-weather drumming sessions spontaneously breaking out on Sundays since the 1970s. Wander secluded paths to spot birds and squirrels, and maybe a chipmunk, groundhog or fox. The mountain's other side is green space of a different kind: two huge cemeteries (*see* p. 86), whose picturesque trees, flowers and historic monuments bring a certain charm to quiet strolls.

This whole area's ideal for pleasant retreats, including the neighbourhoods on Mont Royal's sprawling southern and western slopes: Outremont (the other side of the mountain), a leafy residential area with up-and-coming dining on Van Horne and Bernard avenues; and Côte-des-Neiges (snowy slope), where you'll hear Saint Joseph's bells and a hundred different ethnic communities' conversations.

Métro stations: Peel, Guy-Concordia, Outremont, Édouard-Montpetit, Université-de-Montréal, Côtes-des-Neiges, Snowdon, Côte-Sainte-Catherine, Plamondon, Namur

→ *A quiet autumn moment in Notre-Dame-des-Neiges Cemetery*

SIGHTS
1. Kondiaronk Lookout
2. Saint Joseph's Oratory
3. Notre-Dame-des-Neiges Cemetery

SIGHTS & EATING
4. Beaver Lake Pavilion

EATING & DRINKING
5. Gibeau Orange Julep
6. Le Paltoquet
7. Alma
8. No. 900

1 KONDIARONK LOOKOUT

1196 Voie Camillien-Houde,
Mont Royal
514 843 8240
www.lemontroyal.qc.ca
Open 24-hours
[MAP p. 161 D2

Sure, it's one of Montréal's touristy places, but the panoramic view from Mont Royal's main lookout, or belvédère, is magnifique. Kondiaronk, named after a 16th-century Huron chief, reveals the Saint Lawrence River and some mini-mountains far off in an otherwise flat landscape. Downtown's skyscrapers seem close enough to touch. Day and night, people gaze out and pose for selfies by the lookout's long balustrade. It never feels crowded though, thanks to the large plaza where you can play an old piano, chill on colourful Adirondack chairs, indulge at the ice-cream cart, or ping coins into the giant-bubble-making busker's hat. Then step into the chalet, a Great Depression make-work project. This huge hall is usually dim and empty, and the cafeteria's food is rudimentary, but the big carved squirrels in the rafters and dated murals depicting French colonisation are worth seeing, or you can warm yourself by the wintertime fire.

POCKET TIP
A short walk from the lookout is Mont Royal's famous cross, an illuminated modern edition of the wooden 1643 original.

2 SAINT JOSEPH'S ORATORY

3800 Chemin Queen Mary,
Côte-des-Neiges
514 733 8211
www.saint-joseph.org
Open daily 6am–9pm
[MAP p. 160 A3]

Rising up from the base of
Mont Royal, Saint Joseph's
is a National Historic Site of
Canada and the country's
largest church. It attracts
Catholic pilgrims from around
the world – some so devout
they ascend the long stairs
leading to it on their knees.
Countless non-believers
have also been drawn to
its monumental Italian
Renaissance-style exterior
since before it was completed
in 1967. The formal approach
always impresses, but I've
never overcome my first
impression of the huge interior
being a bit macabre – Exhibit
A being the preserved heart of
the oratory's founder, Brother
Andre, a holy relic displayed
here since his death in 1937.
Other curiosities include
the crypt's collection of old
crutches and walking sticks,
cast aside after the miraculous
healings credited to this priest
later declared a saint. There are
frequent religious services, and
free concerts, including organ
and carillon recitals.

3 NOTRE-DAME-DE/-NEIGE/ CEMETERY

4601 Chemin de la Côte-des-Neiges, Côte-des-Neiges
514 735 1361
www.cimetierenotredame
desneiges.ca
Open daily 8am–5pm
[MAP p. 160 B2]

Even if you don't usually mope around cemeteries, you'll probably like this one's 19th-century angels and modernist mausoleums among lovely landscaped gardens – spectacular during autumn's colourful show, or when draped in fresh snow. Notre-Dame-des-Neiges (Our Lady of the snow) is Canada's largest cemetery, covering 139 hectares (343 acres) of Mont Royal's western side. Established in 1854, it's now the resting place for more than a million, mostly Catholic, souls. Get a booklet (French only) from the administration building and discover notables like revered poet Émile Nelligan, hockey hero Maurice 'The Rocket' Richard, and the composer of Canada's national anthem, Calixa Lavallée. There are also the graves of politicians whose names adorn Métro stations, streets and parks, including Bourassa, Beaudry and Drapeau, as well as five *Titanic* victims. You might spot some wildlife too, such as raccoons and woodpeckers.

POCKET TIP
The predominantly Protestant Mount Royal Cemetery adjacent is also blessed with famous names, historic funerary design and pleasant landscaping.

4 BEAVER LAKE PAVILION

2000 Chemin Remembrance, Mont Royal
514 843 8240
www.lemontroyal.qc.ca
Open daily, varying hours
[MAP p. 160 C2]

You won't spot beavers at Mont Royal's lake, Lac aux Castors, but the pavilion makes other Canadian adventures easy and affordable. In winter, rent cross-country skis, snowshoes, ice skates and inner-tubes (for zooming down the snowy slope nearby) from here, and hire rowboats in summer. Ice has become dangerously inconsistent on Beaver Lake recently so it's been closed to skaters since 2017, but the refrigerated rink adjacent is a free and reliable winter fixture. There's also easy access to the mountain's 18 kilometres (11 miles) of cross-country ski and snowshoe trails. Upstairs in the pavilion's cafe, glass walls and balcony seating make it a prime spot for watching boats, skaters or a double dose of autumn colour reflected in the lake. Service can be bafflingly slow, even at quiet times, but between the views, potted palms and menu – perhaps melon and prosciutto when it's warm or a Hot-Dog Parisien on chilly days – this cafe is Parc du Mont-Royal's most pleasant place of refreshment.

POCKET TIP
Find Parc du Mont-Royal's legendary Tam Tam hand-drumming sessions on spring-through-autumn Sunday afternoons near the George-Étienne Cartier Monument.

5 GIBEAU ORANGE JULEP

7700 Blvd Décarie, Côte-des-Neiges
514 738 7486
Open daily 8am–3am
[MAP p. 158 A3]

This giant retro fibreglass orange has been the roadside snack stop of choice for millions since opening in 1966. The Montréal institution's story goes back to the original concrete structure built here in 1945, and even further to 1932, when Gibeau Orange Julep (whose secret recipe includes OJ and milk) was first sold at a Montréal amusement park. On the Décarie Expressway and surrounded by parking space, this joint is made for drivers, but there's no shame in strolling over from the nearby Namur Métro station – you can see the big orange sphere from the station exit. You'll see this iconic orange dome emblazoned on the cooler kinds of souvenirs that locals love. So what's on offer besides the famous creamy, sweet drink (literally piped to the counter from somewhere inside the building)? Fast-food classics like burgers and dogs, including veggie versions, and poutine of course. Tuck in at the tables outside, but beware of belligerent seagulls! There'll always be queues out the door.

POCKET TIP
Other good cheap and cheerful options in Côte-des-Neiges include Snowdon Deli and Indian vegetarian restaurant Pushap.

GIBEAU ORANGE JULEP

RESTAURANT

MADE WITH FINEST ORANGES DAILY

DRINK ORANGE JULEP

6 LE PALTOQUET

1464 Ave Van Horne,
Outremont
514 271 4229
Open Mon–Fri 8am–6pm,
Sat–Sun 9am–6pm
[MAP p. 170 A3]

People drive from the other side of town for this patisserie-cum-cafe's dreamy French cakes, tarts and pastries. As for the locals, it's very much #sorrynotsorry as they saunter in for a breakfast croissant stuffed with scrambled eggs or a bowl of café au lait. Le Paltoquet, an ironic name that roughly translates as 'hoity-toity', is not much to look at from the outside, and the slightly dark interior would only be notable for vintage posters – if it weren't for the display case's temptations. French born and trained patissier and owner Laurent Bouteraon doesn't hold back on the butter, so his croissants, whether classic, almond or chocolate, are flaky, fluffy fantasies. The sweet selection is phénoménal, from big fruit tarts to little cakes like the chocolate mousse topped with fresh raspberries. The hot chocolate is rich, creamy and not too sweet – the best in town. Plus, there are imported French food products, including Lu biscuits and Banania chocolate drink powder.

7 ALMA

1231 Ave Lajoie, Outremont
514 543 1363
www.almamontreal.com
Open Wed–Sat 5–11pm,
Sun 3–11pm
[MAP p. 170 B3]

There's nowhere better to enjoy Outremont's tranquil joie de vivre than this wine bar nestled in leafy residential Avenue Lajoie. An instant hit when it opened in 2018, it's best appreciated out on the terrasse during sunny summer afternoons. As locals walk by and the trees whisper in the breeze, it's almost like dining in a friend's front yard. Though the cosy red-brick walled interior is far from a bad fallback position when it's chilly. Either way, you'll get smart wines, mainly private imports from France and Spain, especially Catalonia, and wine-friendly share plates that are flavoursome and often Insta-worthy. The menu's Mediterranean inspired with a strong focus on seafood and handmade pasta. Alma's big on fresh, local ingredients too, from crisp spring asparagus to fish from Québec's Gaspésie Peninsula. It's billed as a wine bar but, except at fully fledged pubs and bars, local laws mean you have to order a couple of dishes to be served alcohol. Who's complaining when the food is this good though.

8 NO. 900

1248 Ave Bernard Ouest,
Outremont
438 386 0900
www.no900.com
Open Sun–Wed 11.30am–10pm,
Thurs–Sat 11.30am–11pm
[MAP p.170 B3]

Are you tired of pizza with too-thick crusts and points that instantly collapse? Enter No. 900, which, since opening in 2014, has been creating Neapolitan-style beauties with minimal, gourmet toppings and puffy crusts slightly charred by flash-cooking in super-hot ovens. This is the original No. 900, but it's been breeding new outlets across the province, so you can get perfect pizza from Old Montréal to Québec City. I can't go past this stylish pioneer nestled into the Art Deco **Outremont Theatre**'s street level. Its vintage-inspired design (which won the City of Montréal's Bureau de Design Jury Prize), from the Parisian streetside terrasse to the sleek tiled interior, makes you feel good even before the pizzas arrive – which will be soon, because they are cooked for just 90 seconds. It takes way longer to choose from the concise menu loaded with ingredients like white truffle oil, fior di latte, spicy organic pancetta and figs.

THE LATIN QUARTER & THE VILLAGE

When it's time to party, it's time to hook up with these next door neighbours: the Latin Quarter and The Village. Like its Paris inspiration, the Latin Quarter is anchored by a university whose students fuel an arty-meets-party vibe. They talk, create and hang out at theatres, cinemas, cafes, restos and bars, which are mostly along Rue Saint-Denis. By day this strip's cheap eateries, including samey chains, make it a bit meh. Then hey, presto! The lights come on and beer flows at rowdy pubs serving cheap stuff by the yardarm and at more laidback craft-brew bars.

The Village, named after New York's East Village, could be the most out and proud precinct on the planet, though sometimes it seems straight folks drawn to its bars and restos have taken over. But when night falls this neighbourhood's queer spirit comes out to play, as clubs crank up the dance anthems and drag queens strut their stuff, and LGBTQI gather from around the world during August's Montréal Pride (Fierté). From May to September the main street, Sainte-Catherine, becomes a pedestrian mall with a joyous canopy of countless coloured balls. Originally an all-pink installation, since 2017 the balls have formed a kilometre-long rainbow flag.

Métro stations: Berri-UQAM, Beaudry, Papineau, Sherbrooke

SIGHTS
1. Jardins Gamelin
SHOPPING
2. Boutique Spoutnik

EATING & DRINKING
3. Le Saint-Bock
4. Le Red Tiger
5. Agrikol
6. Complexe Sky
7. Le Blossom
8. Renard
DRINKING
9. Mado

THE LATIN QUARTER
& THE VILLAGE

1 JARDIN/ GAMELIN

1500 Rue Berri, Latin Quarter
Open daily, May–Sept
[MAP p. 162 C3]

Place Emélie-Gamelin was a
bleak concrete 'park' until it
was transformed into Jardins
Gamelin in spring 2015.
Suddenly, it became one of
the most pleasant places in
town, full of performers, kids,
students, tourists, volunteer
gardeners, office workers, bar
staff, and homeless people
too. Jardins Gamelin returns
every spring, when a non-profit
urban design group brings in
picnic tables, stacks of wooden
palettes, a shipping container
bar-cafe, party lights and fun
stuff like fusball tables and
the stone Gamélite people.
There's also a glasshouse
and raised garden beds,
which an urban gardening
collective plants with herbs
and vegetables that anyone
can harvest. A free program of
workshops and entertainment,
from yoga and salsa classes
to spoken word and circus
performances, DJ sessions and
quiz nights, keep energy levels
hovering between laidback
and upbeat. For me, the most
amazing symbol of this public
space's transformation is
Janet Echelman's massive
suspended net sculpture.
Barely visible by day, it's utterly
mesmerising at night, glowing
red then pink and blue.

POCKET TIP
Just beyond The Village,
another urban dead zone
is seasonally transformed
into a beachy riverside
pop-up park, Village au
Pied-du-Courant.

2 BOUTIQUE SPOUTNIK

2120 Rue Amherst, The Village
514 525 8478
www.boutiquespoutnik.com/
Open Tues–Sat 12pm–5pm
[MAP p. 162 B1]

A stray cat walked into this store one day and has literally never left – not even to go upstairs. Like this kitty called Manouche (meaning gypsy, which is ironic now she's abandoned the streets of Montréal), you too will be reluctant to leave Boutique Spoutnik. Especially if you have a weakness for space age vintage. Named after the first artificial satellite, Sputnik, that futuristic silver sphere with a long antennae launched by the Soviets, this store is filled with sleek, often colourful, sometimes kooky homewares from the 1950s, '60s and '70s. Owner Sylvie Rochon's flawless taste is clear, not only in the vintage tables, chairs, lamps, mirrors and curiosities, like a curvy yellow plastic phone, but also in the way she puts it all together in ever-changing vignettes of style and mood. The fact this store has been around since 1998 says a lot about the quality and distinctive, even unique, offerings. So channel your inner astronaut, even if you only have space in your luggage for something from the jewellery cabinet.

3 LE SAINT-BOCK

1749 Rue Saint-Denis,
Latin Quarter
514 680 8052
www.saintbock.com
Open daily 11.30am–3am
[MAP p. 162 B3]

This easygoing brewpub offers 20-plus options of their own creation and several hundred more from near and far. So their 'Beer Bible' is like *War and Peace* but you want to drink, not read, so maybe focus on the 40 kinds on tap. Perhaps the Malédiction milk stout brewed on site, or a refreshing grapefruit radler from Austria. Whatever you fancy – and there's plenty more besides beer, from spiked coffee to regular iced tea – keep 'em coming, and don't overlook the food menu. They've got pub classics like fish and chips, ribs, wings, fries and burgers covered, and several veg options not limited to salad, but the beery bites are the best. Like mac 'n' cheese made with Le Saint-Bock's own Pénitente brew and four kinds of poutine, each with gravy blessed by a different beer. Cosy up with a pint and hockey on the big screens, or kick back on the sprawling terrasse when the weather's warm.

POCKET TIP

If you're more on the whisky tip, check out the 300-strong selection at L'Île Noire bar a few doors down.

4 LE RED TIGER

1201 Blvd de Maisonneuve Est,
The Village
514 439 7006
www.leredtiger.com
Open lunch Tues–Fri 11.30am–
2.30pm, Sat 11am–2.30pm,
dinner Mon–Thurs 5–10.30pm,
Fri 5–11.30pm, Sat 5pm–3am
[MAP p. 163 D1]

In this American-diner-meets-
Hanoi-bar, with a happy,
noisy vibe more like the latter,
modern Vietnamese street food
and booze are best buddies.
Try beer with spicy braised
pork ribs and green papaya
salad, served in an air-filled
bag that looks set to burst.
Or coconut chicken satay
skewers and mini Vietnamese-
style savoury pancakes with
cocktails – all of which pair
spirits and zingy ingredients
like lime, mint, ginger and
lemongrass. 'Me Love You
Long Time' is what one of
them is called, and how I feel
about this place while sipping
and supping on dishes that are,
almost no matter how long the
wait for a seat, worth it. Le Red
Tiger has been white hot since
opening in 2015, so best book a
table, even early in the week.

5 AGRIKOL

1844 Rue Amherst, The Village
514 903 6707
www.agrikol.ca
Open daily 6pm–12am
[MAP p. 162 C1]

Sure, you knew indie band Arcade Fire is from Montréal, but did you know its frontline members Win Butler and Régine Chassagne not only live in The Village but also own a restaurant here? Agrikol is inspired by Chassagne's Haitian heritage and named for the French-Caribbean style of rum distilled from sugar cane. There's plenty of it flowing here – Haiti's own Barbancourt, of course – including for the Ti Ponch: a bucket of ice, lime wedges, fresh-pressed sugar-cane juice and a quarter, half or full bottle of rum to play with. Yes, this is a place for tropical good times, either in the backyard terrasse on a summer night or inside among turquoise and coral walls and a riot of Haitian artwork. The art, including pieces from the owners' personal collection, is inside and out, as are the catchy Caribbean tunes. The authentic vibe continues with the menu of simple bar food like fried chicken, beans and rice, grilled fish and fried plantain.

POCKET TIP
The good times roll on until late at Ti-Agrikol, the bar and music venue next door.

6 COMPLEXE /KY

1478 Rue Sainte-Catherine Est,
The Village
514 529 6969
www.complexesky.com
Open Sun–Wed 11am–12am,
Thurs–Sat 11am–3am
[MAP p. 163 E1]

Taking up a big corner of real
estate with three levels plus a
rooftop, it's hard to argue with
Sky's claim that it's the biggest
gay club in Canada. All that
space means lots of options,
starting at the street-level bar
and restaurant, which spills out
onto a big streetside terrasse
during the warmer months.
That's lunch sorted, time to
head for the rooftop and soak
in the hot tub, take a dip in
the little pool and sip some
sangria while gazing down at
Rue Sainte-Catherine's endless
canopy of plastic balls, criss-
crossing colourfully above the
street in summertime when
it's pedestrian-only. Between
resto and rooftop there are
two floors of good times: drag
shows early in the evening,
then DJ sets from retro pop
and house to hip hop. Like I
said, options! Despite its size,
Sky is a pretty friendly place,
including toward people not of
the LGBTQI tribe.

POCKET TIP
If you're looking for
queer gear including
cheeky sex toys and
bondage essentials,
sashay into men's fetish
store Chez Priape.

7 LE BLO**ƧƧ**OM

1101 Blvd de Maisonneuve Est,
The Village
514 379 3699
www.leblossom.ca
Open lunch Thurs–Fri
11.30am–2.30pm, dinner
Tues–Wed, Sun 5pm–12am,
Thurs–Sat 5pm–1am
[MAP p. 163 D2]

The centrepiece of this
upmarket but affordable new
izakaya is a life-size faux
cherry tree, forever in pale-pink
blossom, spreading out almost
to the ceiling. There's also
some greenery, but the rest of
the fit-out is a masterclass in
streamlined restraint that's part
traditional Japanese design,
part sci-fi: a long zig-zagging
bar of blonde beechwood,
shiny white-tiled walls and
stools with steel finishes
that look like the future. This
visual elegance continues on
the plate, from pretty petal
garnishes to perfectly sliced
and arranged pieces of fish.
There are nearly 50 sakes,
a few shochus, a handful of
cocktails based around these
two close cousins, a white-
focused wine list, and beers
and whisky from Japan and
beyond. Plenty of reasons
to keep those small- and
medium-sized dishes coming,
like salmon sashimi, karaage
chicken and udon soup that's
a noodly, umami dream. And
to keep on gazing at those
beautiful blossoms.

8 RENARD

1272 Rue Sainte-Catherine Est,
The Village
514 903 0648
www.bar-renard.com
Open daily 3pm–3am
[MAP p.163 E2]

Until this bar opened in 2016, classy cocktails in sophisticated surrounds was something you found in other parts of town. Now, people are coming to this increasingly gentrified precinct to lounge on Renard's curvaceous tan leather banquettes with tipples that are equally ooh la la. The beer focus is on microbrews, wine is organic and biodynamic, gin and whisky are the heroes of a spirit selection that's strictly mid- to top-shelf, and cocktails, like the citrusy, herbaceous Botanique, are thoughtfully hand-crafted. About half of the little food menu is on-trend vegetarian, but then there's nachos with barbecued chicken and pulled pork. Renard's decor makes you want to linger, from the blue leather-padded bar to the washrooms' ostentatious floral wallpaper. Even the terrasse constructed each spring is a cut above: a welcoming wooden alcove with a wheelchair-accessible ramp and touches of greenery. This is a place to sip, snack, chat and feel a little foxy – renard means fox after all.

POCKET TIP

The Village's 1853 Church of Saint-Pierre-Apôtre has a Chapel of Hope dedicated to the victims of AIDS.

9 MADO

1115 Rue Sainte-Catherine Est,
The Village
514 525 7566
www.mado.qc.ca
Open Mon–Thurs 4pm–3am,
Fri–Sun 3pm–3am
[MAP p. 163 D2]

Drag queen Mado Lamotte is a
Montréal icon, whose likeness
is among the famous figures
at the city's (quite upmarket)
wax museum. In 2017, she
celebrated 30 years in high
heels and false eyelashes. The
second half of this glittering
career has been at the helm
of Mado, where the facade's
larger-than-life sculpture of
the hostess-with-the-mostess
confirms her icon status.
Inside, she's often seen DJ-ing,
or MC-ing drag shows. Her
naughty, clever banter is mostly
in French and spiced with
Québécois slang, but Madame
Lamotte doesn't leave English-
speaking audience members
hanging, and of course most
of the songs her ladies lip-
sync to are in English. Their
performances are glamorous,
energetic and suggestive, and
segue into late-night dance-
floor action for all. According
to Mado, more than half the
audience is straight for these
drag shows, which are on
every night except Monday –
sometimes with Mado herself
singing live. In 2018, the magic
expanded to a casual resto
next door.

HOCHELAGA-MAISONNEUVE

Emerging from some slightly seedy doldrums, Hochelaga-Maisonneuve has taken on the mantle of HoMa lately, with only a mild degree of hipster irony. Back in the early 19th century, it was farmland, but as the nearby Port of Montréal expanded, this stretch of the Saint Lawrence River industrialised. During the late 19th and early 20th centuries, wealthy landowners set about creating a model industrial city and oversaw construction of grand public institutions, wide boulevards and, of course, magnificent homes for themselves. Their vision is still on show in the Beaux-Arts architecture of buildings like the public bath, original Maisonneuve Market and the town-hall-turned-library.

The precinct, which experienced a slow industrial decline during the 20th century, got a boost when a futuristic stadium was built as the 1976 Olympic Games centrepiece (see p. 109). Also helping things along is the group of science-and-nature-based institutions in Olympic Park and Maisonneuve Park, collectively known as Space for Life, including the planetarium (see p. 108) and botanic garden (see p. 110). Ongoing development keep them among Montréal's most popular attractions, and the cool shops, cafes, restos and bars springing up in the HoMa hood are good reasons to keep exploring.

Métro stations: Préfontaine, Joliette, Pie-IX

→ Maple syrup at Maisonneuve Market

SIGHTS
1. Planétarium Rio Tinto Alcan
2. Olympic Stadium
3. Jardin Botanique

SHOPPING
4. Kitsch À l'Os … ou Pas
5. Coccinelle Jaune

EATING & DRINKING
6. Atomic Café
7. Le Valois

DRINKING
8. L'Espace Public

1 PLANÉTARIUM RIO TINTO ALCAN

4801 Ave Pierre-de Coubertin, Olympic Park
www.espacepourlavie.ca
Open Sun–Wed 9am–5pm, Thurs–Sat 9am–8pm (summer); other seasonal hours vary.
[MAP p. 174 C2]

Opened in 2013, Montréal's planetarium is eye-catching. The main features of its award-winning, eco-focused design rise up from a living green roof: two monumental tapered cylinders, whose aluminium cladding gleams in the sunlight. These are the projection rooms: traditional Milky Way and Chaos, which has Adirondack chairs and beanbags that look like asteroids. The shows are literally out of this world: either science-focused or more artistic takes on space like the popular *Continuum* and *Aurorae* shows. There's also the previous planetarium's projector and a permanent exhibition that's part interactive fun for kids, part meteorite display. These space travellers' cross-sections are remarkably diverse, from colourful crystal pockets to metal with geometric lattice effects that looks like art. Attention, *Star Wars* fans! Have a close look at the tiny Tunisian meteorite fragment's name.

POCKET TIP
The usually flora-and-fauna-filled Biodôme is due to re-open after major renovations in late 2019.

POCKET TIP
Older design wonders are across the road at Château Dufresne, a 1915 mansion with original interior design features and furnishings.

2 OLYMPIC STADIUM

4141 Ave Pierre-de Coubertin, Olympic Park
514 252 4141
www.parcolympique.qc.ca
Open according to event program, tour and observatory hours vary.
[MAP p. 174 C3]

This flawed masterpiece of Organic Modernism is an amazing sight, whether from miles away or up close. Originally dubbed the Big O, Montréal's main 1976 Olympic stadium soon got a new nickname: the Big Owe. Incomplete for the games, one of the most expensive stadiums ever built wasn't paid off for another 30 years, and never-ending structural problems have cost millions more. This 2026 FIFA World Cup venue's main feature is the world's tallest inclined tower with an observatory near the top of its 175 metres (574 feet). With brilliant views in every direction, it's accessed by a funicular that creeps up the outside of the tower. There are guided tours of the stadium but rarely much happening inside. There's often more action on the stadium's grounds, especially for **First Friday**, Canada's largest gathering of food trucks, from May to October.

3 JARDIN BOTANIQUE

4101 Rue Sherbrooke Est,
Rosemont
www.espacepourlavie.ca
Open daily 9am–6pm (summer);
other seasonal hours vary.
[MAP p. 174 A2]

The first time I visited this garden I was surprised there was an entrance fee, but soon realised it's money well spent. There are 75 hectares (185 acres) to explore, all beautifully landscaped and diverse, including various thematic gardens and greenhouses. There's lots of free programming too, from botanical sketching workshops to music performances. It opened in 1931, and over the past few decades major new developments have included Japanese and First Nations gardens, and the Insectarium, a fascinating mini-zoo of creepy crawlies. The pièce de résistance is **Gardens of Light**, an annual autumn event centred in the Chinese garden, where 1000 lanterns glow and reflect off the lake. There's a fresh theme each year, delivering new large-scale lanterns – from ships to dragons. The 10 interconnected glasshouses are always worth checking out, from tropical rainforest plants to cacti, and the **Butterflies Go Free** experience starting late winter.

POCKET TIP

Jardin Botanique has a cafe and restaurant but picnics are also allowed, so get some goodies from nearby Maisonneuve Market.

4 KITSCH À L'OS ... OU PAS

3439 Rue de la Hochelaga,
Hochelaga
514 242 0062
www.kitschalos.com
Open Wed–Fri 12pm–6pm,
Sat–Mon 12pm–5pm
[MAP p. 175 A3]

Looking for socks with a bagel design? A vintage flamingo ornament? Perhaps a shiny vinyl bag from Montréal's 1976 Olympics? You might find them all here – or maybe not, because stock is always coming and going at this wondrous shop whose name means 'kitsch to the bone ... or not'. There are thousands of temptations across nine rooms, including the basement, which became yet another showroom in 2018. About two-thirds is vintage, or 'pre-possessed' as co-owner Daniel Lauzon puts it. The new stuff is vintage-inspired or kitsch or both, and includes hand-picked creations by 80 individual, mostly local designers. It's like an Aladdin's cave of whimsical treasures, ranging from cute new mugs and humorous cushions to a 1950's electric vibrator. Don't miss the room dedicated to Montréal memorabilia. The owners' friendliness is only topped by their dog, an adorable gentle giant called Windy.

5 COCCINELLE JAUNE

4236 Rue Sainte-Catherine Est,
Maisonneuve
514 259 9038
www.coccinellejaune.com
Open Mon–Wed 11am–6pm,
Thurs–Fri 11am–8pm, Sat–Sun
11am–5pm
[MAP p. 175 C2]

Coccinelle jaune means yellow ladybug – doesn't that just make you think of the sweet, sunny feeling of a carefree day? Stepping inside this store full of gorgeous gifty things makes me feel like that too. Everything here is hand-picked by owner Gabrielle Moffett, whose championing of local designers is clear from all the hand-stamped 'créations Québécois' cards stuck here, there and everywhere. More than 90% of her stock is created in the province, from Jack le Chat jewellery to Jacinthe Brind ceramics. There are cute greeting cards and cushions, scented candles and must-have silk scarves, plus a petite women's fashion boutique at the back, **Folle Guenille**. Its elegantly playful dresses, skirts and tops are proudly 'fabriqué au Québec' by designers such as Myco Anna and Slak, in ways that are kind to people and the environment. Get a double dose of carefree vacation shopping at these two stores in one.

POCKET TIP
HoMa poetry pops up each summer along 'Rue de la Poésie': Avenue Desjardins, between Ontario and La Fontaine streets.

6 ATOMIC CAFÉ

3606 Rue Ontario Est,
Hochelaga
514 500 1905
Open Mon–Fri 8am–12am,
Sat–Sun 9am–12am
[MAP p. 175 B3]

Like a cross between the
Jetsons' kitchen and the
Korova Milkbar from *A
Clockwork Orange*, Atomic
Café is good for retro
relaxation, from breakfast
through to cheeky nightcap.
There's lots to like if you like
space-age decor: curvy white
plastic seats, an atomic-
inspired light fixture, super-
retro spherical TV and radio,
and kitsch ephemera. But its
embrace of the past is more
affectionate than obsessive,
and there's an air of early 21st
century HoMa – especially on
the terrasse in warm weather.
The menu is simple cafe-
meets-classic-diner fare. If
you're feeling nostalgic, there
are Eggos, Poptarts, floaters
and Nathan's Famous hot
dogs. For something more
sophistiqué, try the fresh
pastries, kombucha, espresso,
and toasted or cold sandwiches
filled with quality ingredients,
like apple, walnut, lettuce and
brie. There are also a handful
of beers and the usual spirited
suspects. They come into their
own at night when there might
be a band on the rudimentary
stage or a movie projected on
the wall.

ATOMIC
CAFE

7 LE VALOIƧ

25 Place Simon Valois,
Hochelaga
514 528 0202
www.levalois.ca
Open daily 9am–11pm
[MAP p. 175 B2]

A French resto that would be on everyone's lips if it were in a thoroughly gentrified part of Montréal, Le Valois takes the neighbourhood bistro experience up a couple of notches. Designed by Luc Laporte (whose other notable projects include SAT, *see* p. 31), the smart interior is decked out in cherry wood, with backlit panels of coloured-glass chequers above. During warm weather, the generous terrasse overlooking little Place Simon Valois plaza is the place to be. Half of HoMa seems to descend here for sunny weekend brunches. So make a reservation if you want that First World problem of choosing between two types of brioche French toast, three styles of crepes, oodles of egg dishes – baked in little cocottes, benedicts, omelettes et cetera – and more besides. Options later in the day include luxe-casual duck burger with foie gras and crisp fries. Local ingredients shine, prices are reasonable, the wine list's long yet thoughtful, and the mood is warm, whatever the weather.

8 L'E/PACE PUBLIC

3632 Rue Ontario Est,
Hochelaga
www.lespacepublic.ca
Open daily 3pm–3am
[MAP p. 175 B3]

This is the kind of local brewpub you wish was round the corner from your place. Goldilocks-sized, plus a modest seasonal terrasse out the front. Lots of natural wood, and some local artists' work on the walls that changes every month or so. A few bar snacks, but you're welcome to bring some take-out from elsewhere. The happy hum of conversation, and maybe some live music or a DJ. And beer of course, nicely priced. There are 10 taps, a couple of which are reserved for rotating guest microbrews. The rest showcase L'Espace Public's own, evolving with the seasons and experimentation in the on-site brewery. Maybe get a taste of the owner-brewers' love of Hochelaga-Maisonneuve with the classic Hochelager or the HoMa-meets-Cologne Kölschlaga. Don't worry if you're not getting the beers' often playful French names or you simply don't know what to get – the friendly staff can help. Hey, they'll even pour you something else, like whisky or local cider, if you're not into beer.

POCKET TIP

Choose from 300 craft beers to go at nearby Le Bièrologue, which stocks other local drinks and food too.

117

QUÉBEC CITY

With its centuries-old stone buildings, Baroque statues, French conversation and horse-drawn carriages on cobblestone streets, the province of Québec's capital is a piece of the Old World in the new. One of North America's oldest European settlements, its still-fortified heart is a UNESCO World Heritage Site. Some buildings in Old Québec's winding, narrow streets date back to the period when this was the capital of New France, a vast colony stretching south to New Orleans and west into the wilderness. The town began by the Saint Lawrence River in 1535, in what's now Basse-ville (Lower Town). Here, in picturesque Place Royal, the flamboyant bust of Louis XIV shows just how venerable Québec City is. The settlement soon expanded to the clifftop above: Haute-ville (Upper Town), where Château Frontenac (*see* p. 127) was built in 1893. Reflecting Old, or Vieux Québec's enduring Gallic heritage, this fairytale-castle hotel of spires, steeply pitched roofs and tall chimneys dominates the skyline for miles around, and is apparently the world's most photographed hotel.

Unless your tastes are strictly modern, this city's historic charm is irresistible. It's the epicentre of traditional Québécois cuisine, which adapted rustic French cooking to local ingredients and frigid winters, so dine old school at least once.

There are frequent flights, buses and trains between Montréal and Québec City. It's a three-hour journey from Montréal by car, or by public transport to Gare du Palais bus and train station. So a daytrip's possible, but this much charm demands a night or more.

→ *Château Frontenac dominates the skyline of Old Québec*

QUÉBEC CITY

POCKET TIP

The Plains of Abraham, where Britain defeated France in 1759, is now Battlefields Park, an all-seasons public pleasure zone.

Escalier Frontenac

QUÉBEC CITY SIGHTS

Begin exploring Québec City by wandering around the compact old town, poking your nose into venerable churches like **Notre-Dame Cathedral** (16 Rue de Buade, *see* map 179 A2) and **Notre-Dame-des-Victoires** (32 Rue Sous le Fort, *see* map 179 B2), and catching different views of **Fairmont Château Frontenac** (*see* p. 127). One of the most postcard-worthy panoramas is from **Parc du Bastion-de-la-Reine**, beside the **Citadel** (1 Côte de la Citadelle, *see* map 177 E3). Part of the five kilometres (three miles) of fortifications around Old Québec begun in 1620, this star-shaped fort was built by the British during the early 19th century. It's still a military base, with a daily Buckingham Palace-style Changing of the Guard ceremony in summer. Parks Canada run inexpensive, informative guided walking tours of the Citadel and fortifications, as well as the ruins of 17th–19th-century government buildings now under **Terrasse Dufferin**. This broad boardwalk overlooking the Saint Lawrence River is popular for summertime strolls, while in winter its 1884 triple-lane wooden toboggan run is great group fun.

There are several history museums within walking distance, including the **Musée de la Civilisation** (85 Rue Dalhousie, *see* map 179 C1), where the permanent *People of Québec … Then and Now* exhibition is an intriguing summary of the city and province in 350 objects. The smaller **Musée des Ursulines** (12 Rue Donnacona, *see* map 178 C4) is a revealing snapshot of local history in buildings that date from the 17th century. An austere interior reflects that it was once a convent cloistered until 1965, and North America's first school for girls. The intimate chapel and gardens are also open in summer.

There's more to explore just outside the city wall, which is in perfect repair, with four entrances enlarged and rebuilt in the Gothic style during the 19th century. The majestic Second Empire-style **Hôtel du Parlement** (1045 Rue des Parliamentaires, *see* map 181 B2), where the province of Québec is governed from, has frequent free tours (in English and French) of the palatial interior, including the two legislative chambers. The **Musée national des beaux-arts du Québec** (179 Grande Allée Ouest, *see* map 178 C4) is close by, showcasing centuries of Québécois art. Highlights include the collection of works by 20th-century artist

Jean-Paul Riopelle, sculptures by Inuit people of the Arctic, and David Altmejd's wild room-sized installation, *The Flux and the Puddle.*

Accessible by road or the Corridor du Littoral, a 48 kilometre (30 mile) path for walkers, cyclists and in-line skaters, **Montmorency Falls** (5300 Boulevard Sainte-Anne) is at the north-western edge of town. Higher than Niagara Falls, it's worth seeing from multiple angles, including the footbridge, base lookout, cable car and zipline. In winter, spray freezes into a massive cone that, along with the frozen rockfaces on either side, can be climbed with the right equipment. You can snowshoe and hike in the surrounding park too, though **Jacques-Cartier National Park**, just north of Québec City, is a better option, with coniferous forest giving way to vistas of mountains and valleys. Other all-Canadian pursuits here include cross-country skiing and canoeing. Gear can usually be rented within the province's parks, otherwise you'll find sports equipment businesses nearby.

Village Vacances Valcartier (1860 Boulevard Valcartier, Saint-Gabriel-de-Valcartier) is a waterpark in summer then North America's largest winter playground. Streak down snowy slopes in a custom inner-tube, supercharge the

experience on the 34-metre (112-foot) Everest slide, and get your posse into an inflatable raft to bounce or spin across the snow at speed. It's my all-time favourite place to be in winter. Close by, from January to March, is the **Hôtel de Glace** (1860 Boulevard Valcartier). Constructed each winter from densely packed snow and ice carved into bricks, columns, furniture, chandeliers and sculptures, the design is unique each year. It's not just open to overnight guests – guided tour options include a cocktail package, which gets you a drink in a cup made of pure, transparent ice. Go at night when lighting effects make the interior's snowy surfaces glow and ice gleam through the colours of the rainbow.

Yet another reason to visit during the season of snow and ice – quite apart from the fairytale old town's Christmas lights and decorations – is **Carnaval de Québec**. Held in late January and early February, it's one of the world's oldest and largest winter festivals, with everything from snow sculptures to a 'snow bath' – which is OK to watch if you're not game to be among the crazy folks jumping around in the snow wearing swimsuits.

POCKET TIP

During winter's Carnaval everyone drinks Caribou, a warm mix of red wine, hard liquor (usually whisky), spices and maple syrup.

POCKET TIP

Look for big, colourful outdoor trompe-l'oeil frescoes depicting Québec's history, including on Rue du Petit-Champlain and off Place Royal.

QUÉBEC CITY SHOPPING

Among all those souvenir shops selling the same moose and fleur-de-lis tat, there are some distinctive boutiques worth seeking out in Old Québec. Upper Town's **Le Chapelier** (6 Côte de la Fabrique, *see* map 178 C3) is all about snappy hats, for summer and winter, and **Brousseau Inuit Art Gallery**'s (35 Rue Saint Louis, *see* map 178 C4) authentic contemporary sculptures from the far north are stunning, whether you're cashed up or just looking. Fashion and homewares store **Simons** (20 Côte de la Fabrique, *see* map 178 C3) has been in the same building since 1870. This Québec City success story is always so on-trend that there are more stores elsewhere in town and beyond, from Montréal to Vancouver.

Lower Town's Rue du Petit-Champlain and the other little streets around it is said to be North America's oldest shopping district, and is so appealing you have to stroll around here at some point. Stores worth wandering into include **Red Canoe** (88 Rue du Petit Champlain, *see* map 179 B4) for understated Canadiana clothing and accessories, contemporary jeweller **Jules Perrier** (39 Rue du Petit Champlain, *see* map 179 B3), and **La Petite**

Cabane à Sucre de Québec
(94 Rue du Petit Champlain,
see map 179 B4) for every kind
of maple delight.

A little further along the river,
there are several antique
stores on Rue Saint-Paul, and
the **Marché du Vieux-Port**
(Old Port Market 160 Quai
Saint-André, *see* map 178 B1).
It's a sure bet for money-
saving picnic shopping and
gourmet goodies, including
Québec's nectar of the gods,
ice cider, and maple treats,
of course. For high-end
epicurean products, make
a beeline for **J.A. Moisan**
(699 Rue Saint-Jean, *see*
map 181 A1) in Saint-Jean-
Baptiste. It's North America's
oldest grocery store, a claim
that's easy to believe among
the vintage music, old-timey
signs, woodwork and baskets.
They sell the finest foods
from near and far, like local
cheese and Himalayan rose
salt. Nearby find several shops
selling music and books, old
and new, to help your French
along. Independent fashion
store **Point d'exclamation**
(762 Rue Saint-Jean, *see*
map 181 A1) has mostly
Québec-designed women's
apparel and accessories, all
presented with flair.

In Saint-Roch, the city's
modern downtown, local and
international brands gather
along Rue Saint-Joseph.
John Fluevog (539 Rue
Saint-Joseph Est, *see* map
180 C1) is heaven for anyone

POCKET TIP
The short ferry ride across the Saint Lawrence River to Lévis delivers epic views of Old Québec.

who craves head-turning, vintage-inspired shoes and boots, while steps away, **Benjo** (550 Boulevard Charest Est, *see* map 180 C1) is heaven for children. Even if you're not shopping for quality toys from board games to remote-control cars, the big kid in you will want to meet life-size robot Monsieur Bidule and ride the electric train around the store.

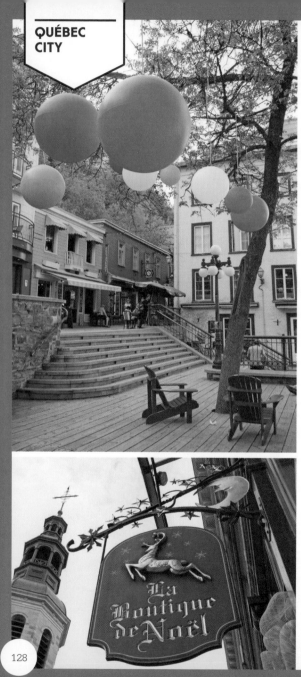

QUÉBEC
CITY

QUÉBEC CITY EATING AND DRINKING

This city serves a variety of food, but does old and new Québecois fare best. **Aux Anciens Canadiens** (34 Rue Saint-Louis, *see* map 178 C4) is an enjoyably authentic place to try Québec's traditional meaty comfort foods (though I'm not sure how authentic the waitresses' very off-the-shoulder period costumes are). The city's oldest house, a red-gabled charmer built in 1675, is filled with antiques, reproduction tableware and hearty dishes like caribou, deer and beef tourtière (pie), bison tenderloin with wild berry sauce, and three maple desserts. Skip the tourist prices with the $20 daytime table d'hôte (host's table) menu.

Steps away, **La Buche** (49 Rue Saint-Louis, *see* map 178 C4) does local comfort food with a more cabin-in-the-woods hipster attitude. Dishes like rabbit wings, poutine, pork rinds, salmon pie and one of the most caramelicious poudings chômeur (unemployed puddings) I've had, all made merrier with Québécois craft beer, cider and fresh tunes.

Even though it's in Upper Town's tourist central, when it's beer o'clock I'm drawn to **Saint Alexandre Pub** (1087 Rue Saint-Jean, *see* map 178 C3) because they have a huge list of brews from Canada

QUÉBEC
CITY

and beyond. In Lower Town, at the bottom of the Escalier Casse-Cou, or Breakneck Stairs, **Rue du Petit-Champlain**'s diminutive scale and historic architecture has made this laneway a tourist honeypot of little boutiques and quaint eateries. It's undeniably enchanting if not too crowded, especially when decked out for Christmas. If you feel compelled to eat here, cute **Cochon Dingue** (46 Boulevard Champlain, *see* map 179 B3) does tasty French bistro fare like onion soup, croque monsieur and bowls of hot chocolate.

A world away, in a pocket of Vieux Québec that tourists rarely go, the **Augustine monastery**'s restaurant (77 Rue des Remparts, *see* map 178 B2) has a tranquil atmosphere and healthy food: salads, soups and simple dishes of game, meat, fish and vegetables that are often local and organic. Bless. They have $18 lunch combos, but for something well priced, quick and potentially sinful, sneak into **Paillard**. This chain of reliably good bakery-cafes, including in Old Québec (1097 Rue Saint-Jean, *see* map 178 B3), has fast French bites, like baguette sandwiches, pastries and macarons.

Fairmont Le Château Frontenac (1 Rue des Carrières, *see* map 179 A3) is a Québec City essential:

even if staying overnight isn't within budget, a drink or well-chosen meal surely is. Recent top-to-toe renovations have introduced contemporary glamour to this grande dame's storied interior, especially in the wining and dining spaces with epic river views. Live it up for a while in the **1608** wine and cheese bar or with a well-crafted cocktail at **Bistro Le Sam**, which also does bar snacks and smart-casual fare like rich clam chowder. The main restaurant, **Champlain**, is baronial grandeur meets 21st-century chic with a menu of regional haute cuisine, from Gaspésie snow crab to Marieville foie gras. This is expensive special occasion territory, or get smart with the $42 treat-filled afternoon tea or $60 Sunday brunch. Reservations recommended.

Between lack of time and Vieux Québec's charms, most visitors don't stray outside the wall. Yet just beyond are **La Grand Allée**'s (*see* map 181 A3) gracious 19th-century houses, which have been turned into the city's most fashionable dining and nightlife strip. **L'Atelier** (624 Grande Allée Est, *see* map 181 A3) is the place for classy cocktails with tapas, tartares and oyster shooters, or there's more affordable fun at **L'Inox** (655 Grande Allée Est, *see* map 181 A3), a brewpub with beer-friendly food including deluxe hot dogs.

Two former working-class neighbourhoods also just beyond the fortifications, Saint-Jean-Baptiste and Saint-Roch, have evolved into lively playtime districts. In slightly bohemian Saint-Jean-Baptiste, **Le Sacrilège** (447 Rue Saint-Jean, *see* map 180 C4) is worth visiting just for their amusing sign. This restaurant-bar has a relaxed, well-worn character, microbrews and pub food, which means good times on the streetside and rear courtyard terrasses, or the old church pews inside. Gourmet burger joint **Chez Victor** (145 Rue Saint-Jean, *see* map 180 B4) is also a favourite with locals, including vegetarians overjoyed by the five burger options. In Saint-Roch, where students and tech entrepreneurs hang, rustic-chic French bistro **Le Clocher Penché** (203 Rue Saint-Joseph Est, *see* map 180 A2) does decadent but good-value brunch plates. **Le Croquembouche** (225 Rue Saint-Joseph Est, *see* map 180 A2), surely the best boulangerie-patisserie in town, has scrumptious cakes, pastries and baguette sandwiches, while brewpub **La Barberie** (310 Rue Saint-Roch, *see* map 177 D1) is the neighbourhood's top beer spot – try all eight on tap with the carousel sampler.

MONT TREMBLANT

Just two hours by car or bus north of Montréal, the Laurentian mountains offer you a deep dive into nature with picturesque towns scattered among forested peaks, rivers and thousands of lakes. Choose from almost every kind of good time in the great outdoors from summer hiking to downhill skiing at the region's 12 resorts.

The biggest of this outdoorsy dozen is Mont Tremblant, which for years has been voted eastern North America's best resort by *Ski* magazine readers. With its mansard roofs, gable windows, pretty colours and pristine paths, Mont Tremblant resort's pedestrian village is a too-nice contemporary take on a Québec town, but from equipment rental to accommodation it aces convenience.

Beyond winter sports, from late spring there are more outdoor activities than you can poke a stick at on and around the mountain. Would you prefer canoeing or white-water rafting? Go-karting or horse riding? The two golf courses are popular, as are the paved cycling paths and trails for mountain and fat bikes.

The Laurentian, or Laurentide, warm-weather grand finale is an endless, undulating sea of fiery autumn colour, which usually peaks around late September or early October. Seeing this natural wonder on a sunny day from the top of Mont Tremblant is a bucket-list experience. After the colour fades, there's a muddy off-peak season until a blanket of snow settles in November, then the mud returns during April and May.

↤ Autumn splendour at Mont Tremblant resort

MONT TREMBLANT SIGHTS

Nestled just inside **Mont Tremblant National Park**, **Mont Tremblant resort** has 14 lifts and 96 ski and snowboard trails on four slopes, plus oodles of other winter fun, like dog-sledding, snowshoeing and tubing, which requires zero skill: just park your butt in the middle of a custom inner-tube and streak down the snowy slope.

A sight to stop you in your tracks from June to October is **Tonga Lumina**, an immersive and interactive nocturnal walk through the resort's forest. This magical mix of story, projections and theatrical lighting effects was conjured by Montréal's Moment Factory, whose other cutting-edge creations include Notre-Dame Basilica's *Aura* (*see* p. 3) sound-and-light show.

Looking for some serious après-adventure relaxation? There are several Nordic-style spas in the area that take you indoors and out, from steam rooms and hot tubs to cold plunge pools. At **Scandinave Spa** a few minutes' drive from the resort, there's the option of taking that cold plunge in the Diable River – which is more adventure than relaxation during winter.

The **P'Tit Train du Nord**, an old train line turned 200 kilometre (124 mile) linear park, is just south-west of the resort and often busy with cyclists and cross-country skiers and snowmobilers in winter. Train stations have been turned into cafes and equipment rental and service centres.

MONT TREMBLANT EATING, DRINKING & ∫HOPPING

After a hard day on the slopes or trails, ice-climbing or rock-climbing, fishing from a boat or fishing through the ice, the scores of places to eat, drink and shop in the resort's pedestrian village are very welcome. **Queues de Castor**'s doughnut-meets-pastry 'beaver tails' are essential sweet snacks. **La Diable** brewpub probably has the most character among the village's many comfort-food and drink options. Its beer is made on-site in gleaming vats, and masses of beer mats are stuck to the walls in a golden-lit space of brick and wood. The **Fairmont Tremblant**'s bars and restaurants are the best bets for indulgence. Treat yourself at this hotel's **Richochet** cafe and terrasse, which is ski-in, ski-out in winter and has a pool and barbecue during summer, or go for broke at the **Choux Gras** brasserie with a

POCKET TIP
Mont Tremblant's summer music festivals include jazz in July and blues in August.

seafood tower to share – that's $105 plus tax and tip. Shop at **Petite Maison Bleue** for cute moose 'n' beaver clothing and gifts, and at all-Canadian apparel brand **Roots**.

For a less manufactured experience than the pedestrian village, or just to avoid the long line of traffic sniffing out resort parking at peak times, check out the original Mont Tremblant township. Connected to the resort by a bike path that becomes a through-town cross-country-ski trail in winter, its offerings include **Restaurant Patrick Bermand**'s refined rusticity and French fare, and **Les Mots Tremblant**, a cosy cafe, wine bar and French and English bookshop.

Mont Tremblant's official downtown area is a little further away. Formerly the township of St Jovite, it's retained some old small-town charm. **Crème et Chocolat**'s hot chocolates are priceless in chilly weather, and **Microbrasserie Saint Arnould** has good in-house beer and Québécois-style pub grub (so, yes, of course they do poutine). Antiques and other pretty homewares and gifts are displayed with photo-shoot style at **Le Coq Rouge**.

OTTAWA

It became an important mark on the world map almost by chance, but this city has grown into its role as Canada's capital with gusto. Epicentre of the 1st July maple-flag frenzy that is Canada Day, it's also home to major national cultural institutions and grand 19th-century buildings constructed in the decades after Ottawa's rise to prominence. There's great eating, drinking and shopping too, thanks to an outlook that's both patriotic and international. From the homegrown beaver tail pastry to globally inspired fine dining among the best I've experienced anywhere, you won't go hungry. Far from being a dreary town of politicians, diplomats and bureaucrats, Ottawa has an outdoorsy attitude evident on the river, canal, parks and wide streets created when this town was planned almost from scratch.

What became Ottawa was mostly ignored by everyone but the Algonquin people until 1826, when the British began building the 200-kilometre (124 mile) Rideau Canal (see p. 144) here. In 1857, the then backwater called Bytown was Queen Victoria's surprise choice for the newly formed nation of Canada's capital. Halfway between rival cities Toronto and Montréal, it was actually a canny compromise that still makes sense in a country whose official languages are French and English. Ottawa is just on the (mostly English-speaking) Ontario side of the provincial border, but the wider area marketed as the Capital Region embraces some of Québec too. It's actually closer to Montréal than Québec City is.

→ *Ottawa's annual tulip festival in full bloom*

OTTAWA SIGHTS

A major engineering achievement that put this place on the map, the **Rideau Canal** is now a UNESCO World Heritage site. During winter, an eight-kilometre (five mile) section becomes the world's largest ice-skating rink and the centrepiece of February's **Winterlude** festival. Take a skate break at on-ice food and drink stalls before taking in other festival highlights on land, such as ice sculptures and snow slides. From spring to autumn, board a canal sightseeing boat at the dock by the **National Arts Centre**. The canal is especially pleasant when the **Canadian Tulip Festival** blooms in May. There are also regular sightseeing cruises along the Ottawa River, showcasing views of the canal's cascade of lochs, **Rideau Falls**, turreted **Fairmont Chateau Laurier** hotel and the grand Gothic Revival **Parliament** building (*see* below). They depart from the base of the lochs and from the other, Québec side of the river, near the **Canadian Museum of History** (*see* p. 148).

The seat of Canadian government, **Parliament** is Ottawa's most prominent landmark: look for the 92-metre (300-foot) clock tower for instant orientation, and listen for chimes that sound

POCKET TIP
Ottawa's biggest
infrastructure project
since the Rideau Canal,
the new electric light
rail Confederation Line
includes three underground
downtown stations.

like London's Big Ben. It's the backdrop for 1st July Canada Day celebrations, including a military parade by Buckingham Palace-style guards, kilted bagpipers and the famous Mounties, as well as summer's daily Changing of the Guard ceremony. Guided tours of the tower and the rest of the main building are off the schedule until major renovations are completed in 2028, but continue elsewhere in the Parliament Hill complex. Tickets for these free tours are available nearby at 90 Wellington Street.

Get a cracking view of Parliament from the **National Gallery of Canada** – though arachnophobes be warned, you have to get past the giant spider sculpture outside the entrance first. Its international collection includes the likes of Rembrandt, Turner and Van Gogh, but don't miss the Canadian collection – especially paintings by the pioneering Group of Seven, who interpreted Canadian landscapes with striking colours and forms in the 1920s and '30s, and Arctic Inuit artists' sculptures in stone, bone and tusk. The gallery recently integrated Indigenous and non-Indigenous art in the Canadian rooms – because it's all Canadian. The free **Ottawa Art Gallery**, which re-opened in 2018 after major renovations, also has a significant Group of Seven collection.

POCKET TIP

The oversize Ottawa sign at ByWard Market's edge (corner of York Street and Sussex Drive) is a top photo op.

The **Canadian Museum of History**, across from Parliament on the other side of the Ottawa River, is the country's most visited museum. If you don't have all day, prioritise the Canadian History Hall, which skips through 15,000 years, and the permanent First Nations exhibition, particularly the boldly designed Pacific coast artefacts. Other major institutions include the **Canadian Museum of Nature** – get hands-on with the new Arctic Gallery's slabs of ice – and the **Canada Aviation and Space Museum**, where open-cockpit biplane joyrides over Ottawa depart.

There's more fresh air in **Gatineau Park**, a big chunk of wilderness a short drive from downtown. Snowshoeing and cross-country skiing give way to hiking, cycling and canoeing (gear can easily be hired in and around the park), plus there's wildlife spotting year-round – I once saw a beaver dam here ... though, sadly, no beavers.

OTTAWA SHOPPING

Maker House Company on Hintonburg's Wellington Street West may have the best selection of luggage-size treasures in town, all handmade by local creatives with a sense of style or humour or both. Why buy a tacky

souvenir when you can get a cool 'Ottawa vs Itself' T-shirt or sweetly ironic magnet of Canadian Prime Minister Justin Trudeau? Other neat shops on Ottawa's emerging street of cool include vinyl oasis **The Record Centre** and wanderlust destination **World of Maps**.

Back in the heart of town, **ByWard Market** is loaded with shopping options. Browse the stalls, then head inside to permanent shops like **John Fluevog**, where Canadian-designed shoes and boots have a pinch if not a generous splash of panache. Also seek out **Milk**'s two floors of curated independent design. It's mostly women's fashion ranging from simple to simply irresistible, plus accessories, jewellery, cards and gifts – including lots of feline flights of fancy.

Close by, the four-level **Rideau Centre** has 180 stores, from international luxury brands like **Tiffany & Co** and **Coach** to national treasures such as **Matt & Nat**. Their chic bags and purses just happen to be vegan, with linings made from recycled bottles. I can vouch for their durability through years of sun and snow. A little further along in Canada's first pedestrian mall, Sparks Street, **The Snow Goose** has been selling authentic First Nations arts and crafts for decades. From beadwork and dream-catchers to Iroquois masks

149

and Inuit sculpture, these are unique keepsakes to treasure.

OTTAWA EATING & DRINKING

Ottawa is the birthplace of beaver tails. These big, thin, crispy doughnuts with sweet toppings are at **BeaverTails** shops around town, including at **ByWard Market** (also *see* p. 149). More district than market – though there are scores of stalls selling produce and curiosities – the capital's eating and drinking hot spot gets lively at night as people descend for fast food, casual meals and relaxed drinks. The self-described 'locally famous' **Zak's Diner** is an Ottawa institution, serving foot-long dogs and super-creamy milkshakes 24/7. **Lowertown Brewery** has several of its own beers on tap, and a menu of beer-friendly food like warm pretzels, burgers and, on Thursdays, buck-a-shuck oysters.

Beyond the market, there are more really good restaurants than you might expect in a city of less than a million people (probably thanks to all those politicians and diplomats). Restaurants like **Riviera**, where the best place to park yourself is the long brass bar running almost the length of this huge heritage bank building. You can indulge on a budget with a glass of

wine and the mushrooms on brioche toast with truffle shavings and runny egg. **Fairouz** has a smart modern Middle Eastern grazing menu and cocktails with ingredients from the souk, like sumac and pomegranate molasses. **Beckta**, a dining room and wine bar in an elegantly renovated 19th-century townhouse, is my Ottawa special occasion favourite, serving superb contemporary Canadian cuisine. They also have a budget-friendly outpost, **Play Food & Wine**.

If you have a few days in Ottawa, or just want to get a taste of life beyond the city centre, check out Hintonburg. This neighbourhood has gone from down and out to hip lately, with foodie destinations popping up along Wellington Street West. **Suzy Q Doughnuts'** fat, fluffy treats come in rotating flavours like maple-bacon and London Fog; **Stella Luna Gelato Cafe**'s flavours are as intense as they are delicious; and **Art Is In** makes beautiful sweet and savoury baked goods to eat in or to go, at what's been described as the ugliest building in Ottawa. All this and more is sampled on **C'est Bon's Hintonburg walking tour**. Bookings essential at www.cestboncooking.ca.

GETTING TO MONTRÉAL

To and from Pierre Elliott Trudeau International Airport

The airport is about 20 kilometres (12 miles) west of downtown.

Bus

The cheapest way to get into town is by the reliable 747 Express bus, which operates 24-hours. Buy a pass from the Société de Transport de Montréal (STM) ticket machine in the international arrivals area. The $10 day pass (24-hour) is the cheapest option for the 747, but three-day, weekend, weekly and monthly passes are also valid and all are good for the metropolitan bus and Métro network. Allow about an hour to get to downtown, though it's faster outside peak times. Unless your accommodation is close to the second and final stop at the bus terminal (gare d'autocars) near Berri-UQAM Métro station, consider getting off at the 747's first stop, Lionel-Groulx Métro station. Your destination is probably accessible by Métro, so get onto this efficient system sooner and avoid downtown traffic. The 747 departs from both Berri-UQAM and Lionel-Groulx for the return journey.

Taxis and other cars

Metered taxis are available at a dispatcher-managed rank outside the international terminal. The fixed downtown fare is $41, and the journey takes about 30 minutes in moderate traffic. Uber pick-ups are outside door six. Limousines, hotel shuttles and rental cars are also available.

Inter-city train

The ViaRail train network links Montréal to many Canadian destinations, including Ottawa and Québec City. The Amtrak train between New York and Montréal is not recommended as buses are cheaper and faster, and you can assume an arrival time hours after what's advertised. Inter-city trains arrive and depart downtown at Gare Centrale, above Bonaventure Métro station.

Inter-city bus

The bus terminal (gare d'autocars) near Berri-UQAM Métro station is the arrival and departure point for long-distance buses that connect Montréal to places such as Ottawa, Québec City, Mont Tremblant, New York and Boston.

GETTING AROUND MONTRÉAL

Montréal is a great walking city, especially in the centre of town, although watch out for paths being blocked by construction and frequent roadworks.

Many streets are designated Est (East) or Ouest (West), but this is determined by the city's orientation to the Saint Lawrence River rather than the compass. The north-south dividing line is Boulevard Saint-Laurent, from where street numbers go up, both to east and west. So 100 Ave Mont-Royal Est is a very different address to 100 Ave Mont-Royal Ouest. Another handy tip is that the ground slopes down from Mont Royal to the river, so in downtown walking down the slope generally means you're going south according to the city's traditional orientation, or south-east by the compass, toward Old Montréal.

Métro and bus

The STM operates the buses and Métro, the city's 68-station underground train network. Most places worth checking out in Montréal, including everything in this book, are easily accessible by this subway system with four colour-coded lines. The Métro operates 5.30am–12.30am daily, or until about 1am on Saturdays.

The STM network's basic paper tickets include single trips ($3.25), but more options are available with the non-rechargeable paper Occasionnelle card, including the three-day pass ($19), and even more with the $6 rechargeable plastic Opus card, including 10-trip ($28) and weekly (Monday–Sunday, $26.25). They are available from ticket booths and vending machines at Métro stations, as well as points of sale listed at www.stm.info/en.

Although some Métro stations look a little worse for wear, it's a safe, reliable system that's had new trains progressively introduced since 2016. Don't bother running to catch one at peak times: there will likely be another in a few minutes. There's usually a train every 5 minutes or so at other times, or about every 10 minutes on weekends.

Elevators are gradually being retro-fitted at stations, but so far only 13 have been installed on one line, the Orange. Elsewhere travellers with mobility issues will struggle to access the system because stairs are ubiquitous – as are heavy doors that even the able-bodied can find difficult to open in windy weather.

The bus network is extensive, including 20-plus routes operating continuously seven days a week, at intervals of four to 45 minutes overnight. Visit the STM website for details and rules for bus transfers with single-fare tickets (avoid this complication by using longer-term tickets, such as the day pass).

Bike

Montréal is one of the world's most bike-friendly cities, with 780 kilometres (485 miles) of cycling paths.

The expansive, inexpensive rental service, **Bixi** (www.bixi.com) has over 6,200 bikes docked at 540 stations and is available 24-hours from April to November. Use credit cards, Bixi membership or a linked STM Opus card at the docking stations' payment machines to access a bike. Options include $2.95 for one trip of up to 30 minutes, $5 for 24-hours, $25 for 10 trips and $32 for 30 days. An electric-bike pilot project launched in 2018.

If you're riding a non-docking bike, be aware that bicycle theft is rife in Montréal (surprisingly for a city that otherwise has a low crime rate). If you leave a bike, lock it very securely.

Cars: rental, sharing and taxi

In Canada you drive on the right side of the road. Speed signs are in kilometres, and most road signs in the province are only in French. It's illegal to turn right at a red light on the island of Montréal but no problem elsewhere. When a green light is flashing, you can turn left.

Tolls have recently been introduced in Québec, on the A30 (pay with cash or credit card at toll booths, or get a transponder) and the A25 (transponder only, or the more expensive 'video tolling' that involves automatic photographing of license plates).

By law, cars must be fitted with snow tyres in winter, when street parking can also become challenging – both despite and because of the city's very active snow-removal program.

There is little danger of encountering wild animals on roads in the cities related to this book. Note that the blood-alcohol limit for drivers is 0.08%.

Rental cars are readily accessible and affordable, except during peak times, such as long weekends and summer break. To rent a car in the province of Québec you must be at least 21 and have had a license (from any country, as long as it uses the Latin alphabet) for at least a year.

Montréal has one of North America's highest rates of car-share usage. **Car2go** (www.car2go.com) and **Communauto** (www.communauto.com) are widely available. Uber is legal, but taxis are still common and reliable, including **Taxi Co-op** (www.taxi-coop.com) and **Téo Taxi** (www.teomtl.com), which uses electric cars.

Boat

A pleasant way to travel between the Old Port and the nearby islands collectively known as Parc Jean-Drapeau is the **Navettes Maritimes shuttleboat** (www.navettesmaritimes.com). Available May to October, it's $4.25 one-way. Sightseeing cruises along the Saint Lawrence River and Lachine Canal also depart from the Old Port. Options include **Croisières AML** (www.croisieresaml.com) and **Le Petit Navire** (www.lepetitnavire.ca).

QUÉBEC SOVEREIGNTY

While many Montréalers are effortlessly bilingual, the division of French and English linguistic and cultural history can sometimes be a sensitive topic. Separatists feel that the French language and other distinctive aspects of the province's culture are not given due respect by the rest of Canada, which is mainly English speaking. If the narrowly defeated referendums held in 1980 and 1995 are any indication, about half of Québec wants to stay part of Canada, and about half wants to form an independent Québecois nation. Fortunately it's easy to get a better understanding of the facts and feelings on the subject, because most Montréalers speak your language.

MONEY

Both cash and credit cards (especially Visa and MasterCard) are accepted, though small businesses may have a minimum spend on cards, and some may only take cash. ATMs (les guichets) connected to the international Cirrus, Maestro and Plus networks are widely available at banks, as well as bars, convenience stores and hotels.

Except at rare places with signs advising taxes included, expect a 5% federal goods and services tax (GST) and Québec provincial tax (TVQ) of 9.975% to be added when it's time to pay. For meals and taxi fares, add another 15% tip to the pre-tax amount, or 20% for exceptional service. A $1 tip per drink, or $2 for cocktails or service above and beyond, is also expected, so keep some $1 and $2 coins (the loonie and toonie respectively) handy. Most restos, cafes and bars have credit-card machines that give you the option of adding tips by percentage or dollar amount.

VOLTAGE

Canada's electricity supply is the same as the United States: 120V/60Hz. Power outlets are for two- or three-prong plugs.

WEATHER

Between May and September, Montréalers are outside as much as possible in temperatures usually hovering in the 20s (celsius, or 70–85F), but humidity often makes it feel warmer. It's not uncommon to get well into the 30s (85–100F), with high humidity producing a Real Feel into the 40s (105–115F). It's also not uncommon to have chilly spells even in the middle of summer.

Winter is changeable too, with periods above freezing, but from December to February expect snow and top temperatures around -5 to -15 (25–5F), though wind and humidity will make it feel colder. Temperatures go lower at night, and even during the day it could easily be -20 (-5F) with an even colder Real Feel. It's usually at least a few degrees colder in Québec City and on Mont Tremblant. It's not only uncomfortable to be inadequately dressed in conditions like this, it's also dangerous. Be prepared: besides hat, gloves and scarf, insulated coat and boots or long thermal underwear are recommended. Freezing temperatures are common in Montréal in March and November, and it's not out of the question to get snow in April and October. Beware of slippery ice from October to April.

It's bleak, cold and muddy in Montréal from when the snow melts in March until spring explodes around mid-May, then again from when autumn's spectacular colour vanishes in late October until the snow sets in around late November or December.

PHONES & WI-FI

The City of Montréal provides one of the world's biggest free public wi-fi networks (MTLWiFi). Many public institutions, from parks to museums, and most restos, cafes, bars and accommodation, also provide free access. There is free wi-fi in Québec City through ZAP Québec, and in Ottawa via Capital WiFi.

Canada's telephone country code is 1. Montréal's area codes are 514 and 438, and must be included when dialling. For local SIM cards, **Fido** (www.fido.ca) and **Koodo** (www.koodomobile.com) are good options.

LANGUAGE

French is the only official language in the province of Québec and the first language for most residents. The majority of Montréalers are fluent in both French and English, and there are also many migrants who speak one or more other languages. Montréal's cashiers and servers often use the greeting 'bonjour hi', which is the cue to choose your language. While customer service workers who don't speak English are rare, it's best not to assume, and at least starting with a few words of French will be appreciated. Outside Montréal, especially beyond tourist zones, French may be the only option.

Even if you're fluent in French, you may have difficulty with the version spoken in Québec. It's rooted in pre-Revolutionary French, because immigration from France stopped when the British took over in 1760. An everyday example is that while breakfast is petit déjeuner in France, it's déjeuner in Québec. Lunch is dîner, not déjeuner, and dinner is souper, not dîner. Many words and phrases borrowed and adapted from British, Canadian and American English, as well as ones born out of the distinctive Québec experience, have been added to this old French over the centuries, so at meal's end ask for le bill, not l'addition.

Useful words and phrases

Hello Bonjour
Goodbye Au revoir
See you soon! À bientôt!
Please S'il vous plaît
Thank-you (very much) Merci (beaucoup)
Yes Oui
No Non
Do you speak English? Parlez-vous anglais?
I don't speak French Je ne parle pas français
I don't understand Je ne comprend pas
Sorry Désolé
Excuse me Pardon
How much does it cost? C'est combien?
Where are the toilets? Où sont les toilettes?
It's good! C'est bon!
Cheers! Santé!

Signs

Welcome Bienvenue
Open Ouvert
Closed Fermé
Women Femmes
Men Hommes
Exit Sortie
Prohibited Interdit
Street closed Rue barré
Stop Arrêt

HOTEL RECOMMENDATIONS

Budget
HI Montréal
Auberge Internationale de Québec
HI Mont-Tremblant
HI Ottawa Jail

Affordably fancy
L Hotel
Hôtel Nelligan
Auberge Place d'Armes
Andaz Ottawa ByWard Market

Luxe
Fairmont The Queen Elizabeth
Fairmont Château Frontenac
Fairmont Château Laurier

TOURIST INFORMATION

Tourisme Québec (www.quebecoriginal.com) promotes travel across the province and has information centres in Montréal and Québec City. There are also info centres operated by **Tourisme Montréal** (www.mtl.org), **Québec City Tourism** (www.quebecregion.com), **Tourism Mont-Tremblant** (www.mont-tremblant.ca) and across the Ontario border by **Ottawa Tourism** (www.ottawatourism.ca).

EATING & DRINKING

Traditional Québecois food is made for comfort. It's centred around meat, especially the pork and beef introduced by French settlers, as well as game like duck and caribou. Classic dishes include large meat pies called tourtière, and two more recent additions: the hot mess of fries, curds and gravy called poutine, and pouding chômeur (unemployed pudding). This simple, warm cakey pudding with caramel sauce is much more than the sum of its simple parts when done right.

Pouding chômeur is sometimes made with maple syrup, another popular local that's in everything from coffee to beer during the March-April harvest. Most of the world's maple syrup is produced in Québec, including at dozens of farms just outside Montréal that open to the public during this 'sugaring-off' season. The communal restaurant meals at these cabanes à sucre, or sugar shacks, are a great way to enjoy traditional Québécois food. A few are open year-round, including the charming Auberge Handfield and Sucrerie de la Montagne.

Waves of migration since the French then British colonial eras have introduced foods from many parts of the world to Montréal. Jewish migrants brought two fast foods that have become synonymous with the city: bagels, which are thinner and crisper than the New York style, and smoked meat, or viande fumée. Similar to British corned beef and New York pastrami, beef brisket is salted, cured and cooked, then served between light rye bread with yellow mustard.

There are many casual vegetarian and vegan eateries in Montréal, and most cafes and restos – the shorthand for restaurant used by everyone in Montréal – have generous veg options. Dining out in style without meat is challenging though. Fresh seasonal produce is abundant and often outstanding from June to September, especially asparagus, corn and apples from the markets. During the rest of the year most food is imported, and sometimes expensive and worse for wear.

The legal drinking age in Québec is 18. The importation and sale of alcohol is controlled by the Société des Alcools du Québec, whose SAQ stores are the only place you can buy most kinds of booze to go. The exceptions are beer (which is hardly sold at SAQs), cider and cheap wine, available from supermarkets and the ubiquitous dépanneurs: neighbourhood convenience stores.

Craft beer is big and beautiful in Québec. There are more than 150 microbreweries around the province, and many in Montréal operate as brewpubs, or microbrasseries. These bars offer a rotating list of beers, usually made on site, and are a quintessential MTL experience – MTL being common shorthand for the city.

Québec also makes exceptional cider, especially in the apple-growing region of Montérégie directly south of Montréal. There are about a dozen cideries open to the public for tastings and sales here, but quality still, sparkling and ice ciders are easy to find on menus and shop shelves. Ice cider, which is like ice wine but made with apples, is a taste sensation still under-appreciated by the rest of the world. Be sure to try this dessert cider while you're here, as well as the excellent local gins and whiskies.

PUBLIC HOLIDAYS

New Year's Day 1 January

Good Friday and **Easter Monday** are in late March to mid-April, but opening hours aren't usually affected.

Patriots Day, also known as Victoria Day, is on 24 May or the nearest Monday.

Saint Jean Baptiste Day is the province's Fête Nationale, so you will see lots of Québec flags.

Canada Day on 1 July is low key here, partly because leases traditionally end on 30 June so half the city is moving on what's better known as Moving Day.

Labour Day is the first Monday in September.

Thanksgiving is the second Monday in October.

Christmas Day 25 December

MONTRÉAL CITY MAPS

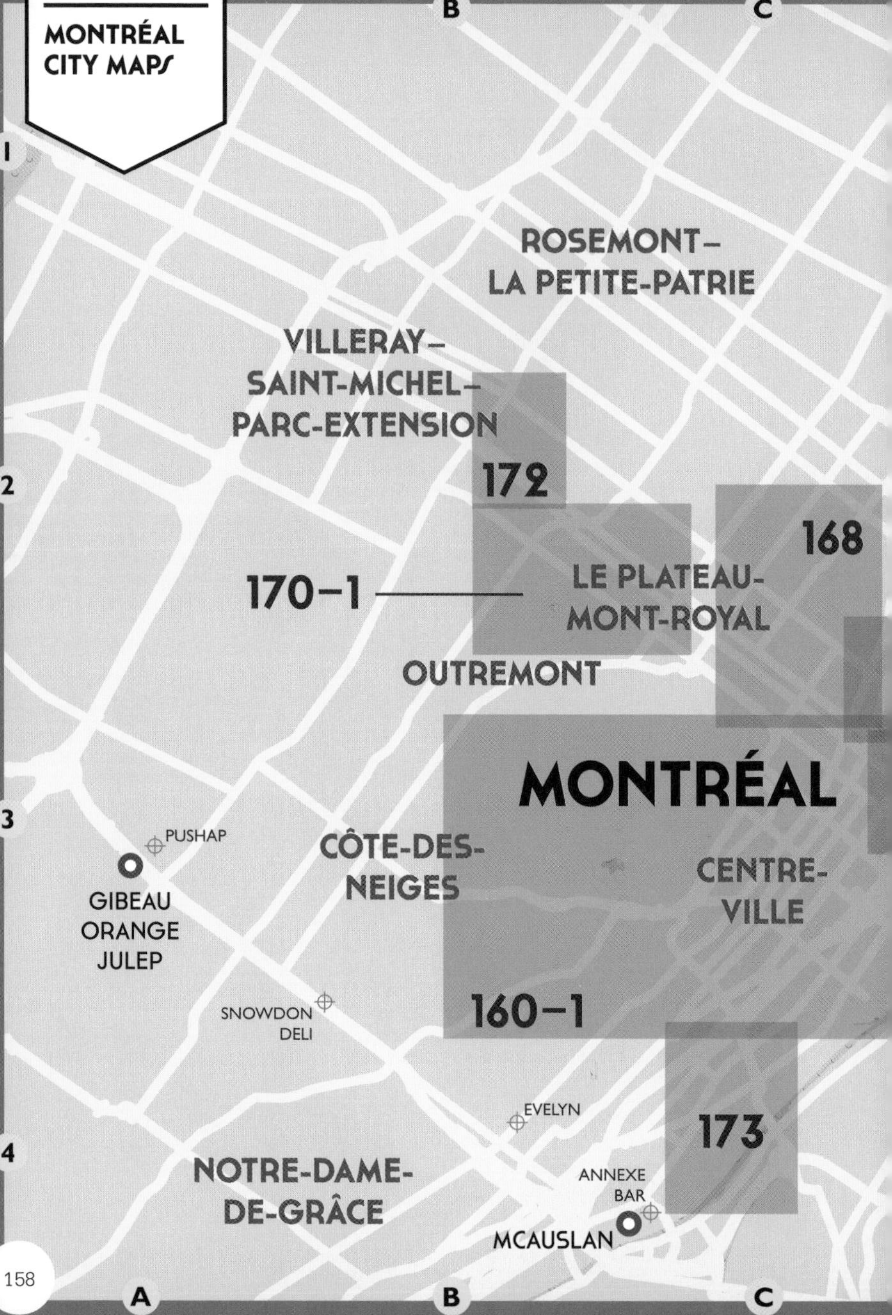
B
C
1
ROSEMONT–
LA PETITE-PATRIE
VILLERAY–
SAINT-MICHEL–
PARC-EXTENSION
172
2
168
170–1
LE PLATEAU-
MONT-ROYAL
OUTREMONT
MONTRÉAL
3
PUSHAP
CÔTE-DES-
NEIGES
CENTRE-
VILLE
GIBEAU
ORANGE
JULEP
SNOWDON
DELI
160–1
EVELYN
173
4
NOTRE-DAME-
DE-GRÂCE
ANNEXE
BAR
MCAUSLAN
A
B
C

D

 NOTRE DAME
DES VICTOIRES

MAISONNEUVE
⊕ MARKET

174

MAISONNEUVE

175

HOCHELAGA

E

F

TO
QUÉBEC
CITY

1

Fleuve Saint-Laurent

2

169

162–3

VIEUX-
LONGUEUIL

164–5

3

PLAGE
⊕ JEAN-DORÉ

GREENFIELD
PARK

166–7

4

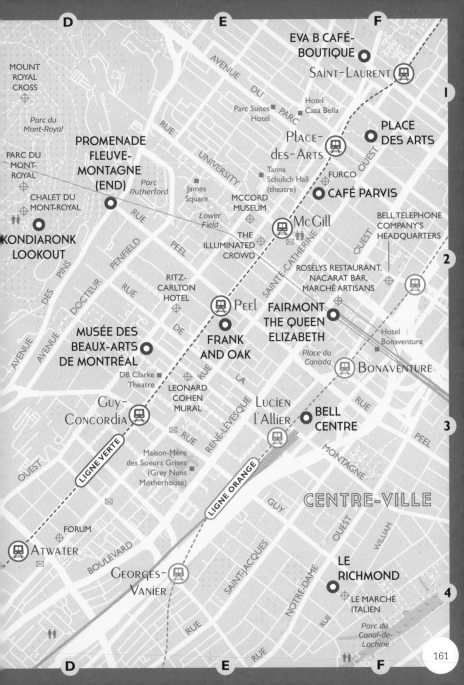

EVA B CAFÉ-BOUTIQUE

Saint-Laurent

MOUNT ROYAL CROSS

AVENUE DU PARC

Parc du Mont-Royal

Parc Suites Hotel

Hotel Casa Bella

Place-des-Arts

PLACE DES ARTS

PARC DU MONT-ROYAL

PROMENADE FLEUVE-MONTAGNE (END)

RUE

UNIVERSITY

Parc Rutherford

James Square

Tanna Schulich Hall (theatre)

FURCO

CAFÉ PARVIS

CHALET DU MONT-ROYAL

Lower Field

MCCORD MUSEUM

McGill

BELL TELEPHONE COMPANY'S HEADQUARTERS

KONDIARONK LOOKOUT

RUE

THE ILLUMINATED CROWD

SAINTE-CATHERINE

ROSÉLYS RESTAURANT, NACARAT BAR, MARCHÉ ARTISANS

DES PINS

PENFIELD

PEEL

RITZ-CARLTON HOTEL

Peel

FAIRMONT THE QUEEN ELIZABETH

Hotel Bonaventure

DOCTEUR

RUE

DE

FRANK AND OAK

MUSÉE DES BEAUX-ARTS DE MONTRÉAL

DB Clarke Theatre

Place du Canada

Bonaventure

AVENUE

AVENUE

LEONARD COHEN MURAL

RUE

LA

RENÉ-LÉVESQUE

Lucien l'Allier

RUE

Guy-Concordia

LIGNE VERTE

Maison-Mère des Soeurs Grises (Grey Nuns Motherhouse)

LIGNE ORANGE

BELL CENTRE

MONTAGNE

PEEL

OUEST

GUY

CENTRE-VILLE

OUEST

WILLIAM

FORUM

Atwater

BOULEVARD

GEORGES-VANIER

SAINT-JACQUES

NOTRE-DAME

LE RICHMOND

LE MARCHÉ ITALIEN

RUE

RUE

Parc du Canal-de-Lachine

D   E   F

BOUTIQUE SPOUTNIK

Écomusée du Fier Monde

AGRIKOL

MONTCALM

WOLFE

ROBIN

AMHERST

RUE

SAINT-ANDRÉ

RUE SHERBROOKE EST

Om Hotel

RUE

SAINT-HUBERT

RUE BERRI

SUSHI MOMO

🚇 Sherbrooke

RUE DE MALINES

Hôtel de l'ITHQ

Crémazie monument

Square Saint-Louis

Auberge du Carre St-Louis (hotel)

Monument Émile Nelligan

SAINT-TIMOTHÉE

Parc Robert-Prévost

ONTARIO EST

SAINT-ANDRÉ

SAINT-CHRISTOPHE

Parc Saint-Jacques

LIGNE ORANGE

RUE BERRI

SAINT-HUBERT

Hotel Elegant

Lelux Hotel

Loft Hotel

LE SAINT-BOCK

L'ÎLE NOIRE BAR

JARDINS GAMELIN

Berri -Uqam 🚇

Parc Émilie Gameli

AVENUE DE

SHERBROOKE EST

RUE SAINT-DENIS

RUE

ONTARIO EST

SANGUINET

Le Relais Lyonnais (hotel)

Cinémathèque Québécoise

Gite du Plateau Mont-Royal (hotel)

Armor Manoir Sherbrooke (hotel)

L'HÔTEL-DE-VILLE

RUE DE BULLION

RUE

BOULEVARD SAINT-LAURENT

SAINT-DOMINIQUE

CLARK

EVA B CAFÉ-BOUTIQUE

Parc Toussaint-Louverture

DE MAISONNEUVE

LIGNE VERTE

BOULEVARD

Parc Paul-Dozois

HENRI HENRI

LE LAB

LE SAINTE-ÉLISABETH

D

E

F

RUE

AVENUE PAPINEAU

EST

Parc
Raymond-
Blain

RUE

RUE PLESSIS

RUE

ALEXANDRE-DESÈVE

RUE DE CHAMPLAIN

DE

PANET

MAISONNEUVE

Parc
Charles S.
Cambell

I

LA

VISITATION

DE

COMPLEXE
SKY

RUE

EST

RENÉ-LÉVESQUE

RUE

RUE

VILLAGE
GAI

RUE

DALCOURT

LE RED
TIGER

Beaudry

CHEZ
PRIAPE

PLESSIS

BOULEVARD

RENARD

RUE

PANET

LE BLOSSOM

Le National
(theatre)

CHURCH OF
SAINT-PIERRE-
APÔTRE

BOULEVARD

EST

2

EST

MADO

BEAUDRY

MONTCALM

RUE

RUE

WOLFE

AMHERST

Olympia
(theatre)

SAINTE-CATHERINE

SAINT-TIMOTHÉE

RENÉ-LÉVESQUE

RUE

SAINT-ANDRÉ

EST

EST

3

Hôtels
Gouverneur
Montréal

BOULEVARD

RUE

RUE DE LA GAUCHETIÈRE EST

VIGER

RUE NOTRE-DAME EST

Hotel
Lord
Berri

SAINT-HUBERT

Maison
Brunet
(hotel)

AVENUE

N

RUE

La Conciergerie
(hotel)

0   200 m

LIGNE JAUNE

BERRI

4

Celebrities
Hotel

Jeanne d'Arc
artwork

Carré
Viger

Forces
artwork

RUE

SAINT-HUBERT

Agora artwork

Mastodo artwork

Square
Dalhousie

D

E

F

A B C

Parc Paul-Dozois

Saint-Laurent

BOULEVARD

LIGNE VERTE

RUE

HENRI HENRI

AVENUE

RUE

DE

Hôtel Chrome

RUE SAINT-DE

RUE

SANGUINET

MTELUS (theatre)

LABO CULINAIRE (FOODLAB)

Candlewood Suites

SAINTE-ÉLISABETH

RUE

Hôtel Faubourg Montréal

L'HÔTEL-DE-VILLE

SATOSPHÈRE

SAINTE-CATHERINE

Place de la Paix

OUEST

DE

CHAMP-de-MARS

Place des Montréalaises

N

PLACE DES ARTS

SAINT-URBAIN

LA SOCIÉTÉ DES ARTS TECHNOLOGIQUES

SAINT-DOMINIQUE

BULLION

OUEST

2

QUARTIER DES SPECTACLES

Hyatt Regency Montreal

RENÉ-LÉVESQUE

RUE

Travelodge Hotel by Wyndham Montreal Centre

SAINT-LAURENT

Parc Sun Yat Sen

VIGER

EST

RUE

RUE

0   200 m

QUARTIER CHINOIS

AVENUE

VILLE-MARIE

Allegrocub artwor

RUE

JEANNE-MANCE

Place d'Armes

SAINT-ANTOINE

Parc de La Presse

TERRASSE PLACE D'ARMES

OU

3

BOULEVARD

DE

LIGNE ORANGE

AUTOROUTE

ALDRED BUILDING

NOTRE-DAME BASILICA

NOTRE-DA CATHEDR

BLEURY

Hôtel le Dauphin

RUE

SAINT-ALEXANDRE

RUE

Embassy Suites by Hilton

SAINT-JACQUES

SULPICIAN SEMINARY

NOTRE-DAME

Centaur Theatre

Olympic Torch monument

Place Jean-Paul-Riopelle

InterContinental (hotel)

4

BELL TELEPHONE COMPANY'S HEADQUARTERS

TOQUÉ!

Hotel le St-James

L HOTEL

VIEUX-MONTRÉAL

164

Square-Victoria-OACI

A B C

ne d'Arc
twork

D

Agora
artwork

Mastodo
artwork

RUE EST

RUE

E

Du Chemin
Qui Marche
(view point)

F

PLAGE
D'HORLOGE

THE OLD PORT'S
CLOCK TOWER

I

Square
Dalhousie

BERRI

SAINT-ANTOINE

LIGNE JAUNE

EST

NOTRE-DAME-
DE-BON-SECOURS
CHAPEL

EST

SAUTE MOUTONS
JET BOATING

PETITE MAISON
BLEUE PAR HATLEY

RUE GOSFORD

Champ-
De-Mars

LA CHAMPAGNERIE

RUE DE LA COMMUNE

RUE DU QUAI-DE-L'HORLOGE

Vieux-
Port

TYROLIENNE
MTL ZIPLINE

CHAMP DE
MARS PARK

NOTRE-DAME

MARCHÉ
BONSECOURS
BUILDING

BONSECOURS
BASIN

2

Place De La
Dauversière

VOILES
EN VOILES

Place
Marguerite-
Bourgeoys

TERRASSE
WILLIAM
GRAY

RUE SAINT-VINCENT

THE
COLDROOM

RUE DE LA COMMUNE

LA GRANDE ROUE
DE MONTRÉAL

TERRASSES
BONSECOURS

NAVETTES
MARITIMES

RUE SAINT-GABRIEL

QUEUES
DE CASTOR

DÉLICES
ÉRABLE & CIE

EST

TERRASSE SUR
L'AUBERGE

3

TAVERNE GASPAR

Les
Chuchoteuses
artwork

SAINT-PAUL

Vieux-
Port

RUE DU QUAI KING EDWARD

Saint-Laurent

Le Saint-Sulpice
(hotel)

TERRASSE
NELLIGAN

DÉCALADE

PETIT
P

POINTE-À-
CALLIÈRE

PROMENADE
FLEUVE-MONTAGNE
(START)

Fleuve

4

D

E

F

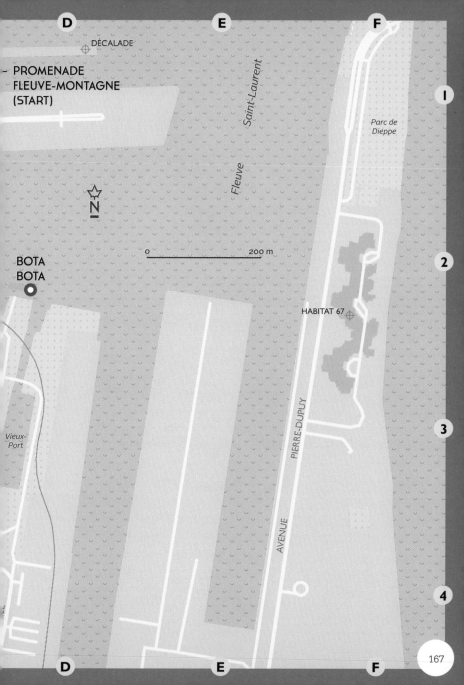

D

E

F

DÉCALADE

– PROMENADE FLEUVE-MONTAGNE (START)

Saint-Laurent

Parc de Dieppe

I

Fleuve

N

0 ———————— 200 m

2

BOTA BOTA

HABITAT 67

3

PIERRE-DUPUY

Vieux-Port

AVENUE

4

167

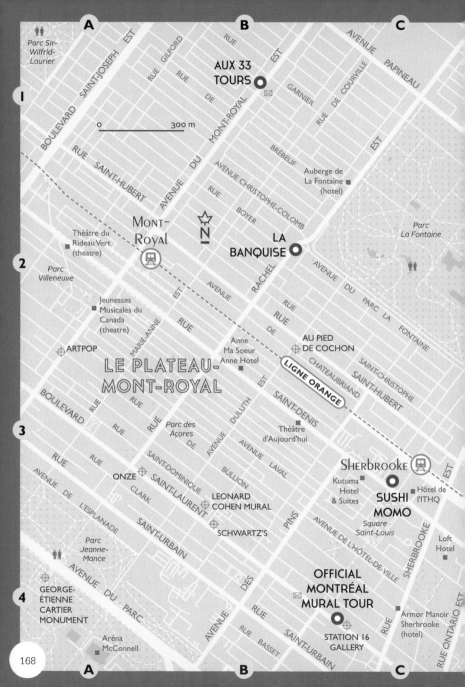

A ··· Parc Sir-Wilfrid-Laurier

B

C ··· AVENUE PAPINEAU

1

BOULEVARD SAINT-JOSEPH EST

RUE GILFORD

RUE

RUE DE

AVENUE DU MONT-ROYAL

RUE

GARNIER

RUE DE COURVILLE

EST

AUX 33 TOURS ✉

RUE SAINT-HUBERT

AVENUE CHRISTOPHE-COLOMB

BRÉBEUF

EST

RUE BOYER

Auberge de La Fontaine (hotel) ■

300 m

Mont-Royal

Théâtre du Rideau Vert (theatre) ■

☆
N

LA BANQUISE ◉

Parc La Fontaine

2

Parc Villeneuve

AVENUE DU PARC LA FONTAINE

RUE RACHEL EST

Jeunesses Musicales du Canada (theatre) ■

RUE MARIE-ANNE

RUE

RUE DE

AU PIED DE COCHON

RUE SAINT-CHRISTOPHE

RUE SAINT-HUBERT

⊕ **ARTPOP**

LE PLATEAU-MONT-ROYAL

Anne Ma Soeur Anne Hotel ■

CHATEAUBRIAND

LIGNE ORANGE

BOULEVARD

RUE

RUE

Parc des Açores

AVENUE DE

AVENUE DULUTH EST

AVENUE LAVAL

SAINT-DENIS

RUE

3

RUE

RUE

SAINT-DOMINIQUE

BULLION

Théâtre d'Aujourd'hui ■

Sherbrooke 🚇

RUE

ONZE ⊕

SAINT-LAURENT

CLARK

LEONARD COHEN MURAL

RUE PINS

Kutuma Hotel & Suites ■

SUSHI MOMO ◉

Hôtel de l'ITHQ ■

AVENUE DE L'ESPLANADE

SAINT-URBAIN

SCHWARTZ'S ■

Square Saint-Louis

Loft Hotel ■

Parc Jeanne-Mance

AVENUE DE L'HÔTEL-DE-VILLE

SHERBROOKE

4

⊕ **GEORGE-ÉTIENNE CARTIER MONUMENT**

AVENUE DU PARC

AVENUE DES

RUE

RUE

OFFICIAL MONTRÉAL MURAL TOUR ✉

RUE

Armor Manoir Sherbrooke (hotel) ■

Aréna McConnell ■

SAINT-URBAIN

RUE BASSET

◉ ⊕ **STATION 16 GALLERY**

RUE ONTARIO EST

A

B

C

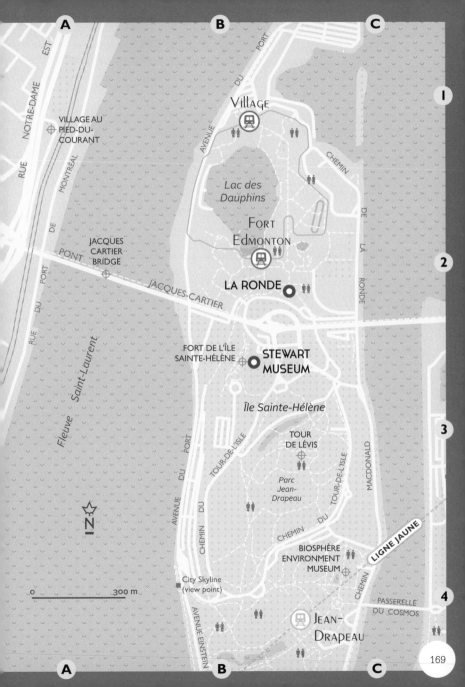

A

RUE NOTRE-DAME EST

VILLAGE AU PIED-DU-COURANT

DE MONTRÉAL

PONT

RUE DU PORT

JACQUES CARTIER BRIDGE

JACQUES-CARTIER

Fleuve Saint-Laurent

N

0   300 m

B

DU PORT

AVENUE DU PORT

Village

Lac des Dauphins

FORT Edmonton

LA RONDE

FORT DE L'ÎLE SAINTE-HÉLÈNE

STEWART MUSEUM

Île Sainte-Hélène

AVENUE TOUR-DE-L'ISLE

TOUR DE LÉVIS

Parc Jean-Drapeau

CHEMIN DU TOUR-DE-L'ISLE

AVENUE DU

CHEMIN DU

CHEMIN

City Skyline (view point)

BIOSPHÈRE ENVIRONMENT MUSEUM

AVENUE EINSTEIN

JEAN-DRAPEAU

C

CHEMIN DE LA RONDE

MACDONALD

LIGNE JAUNE

CHEMIN

PASSERELLE DU COSMOS

1

2

3

4

A
B
C

I

AVENUE

RUE BEAUBIEN OUEST

BOULEVA

RUE

HUTCHISON

DU

N

Parc
Lhasa-
Sela

AVENUE

RUE

JEANNE-MANCE

DE

L'ESPLANADE

2

o   300 m

HORNE

PARC

RUE

LIBRAIRIE
DRAWN AND
QUARTERLY

AVENUE DUCHARME

VAN

AVENUE

AVENUE

AVENUE

HUTCHISON

AVENUE

AVENUE

OUTREMONT

AVENUE

LAJOIE

DE L'ÉPÉE

DUROCHER

Parc
John-F.-
Kennedy

AVENUE

BERNARD

QUERBES

3

ALMA

Parc
Saint-
Viateur

LE
PALTOQUET

OUTREMONT

AVENUE

NO. 900

BLOOMFIELD

Parc
Raoul-
Dandurand

BOULEVARD

AVENUE

Théâtre
Outremont

CHAMPAGNEUR

SAINTE-VIATEUR

LIGNE BLEUE

AVENUE

AVENUE

OUTREMONT

Parc
Outremont

4

AVENUE

MCEACHRAN

STUART

DOLLARD

WISEMAN

AVENUE

OUTREMONT

AVENUE

DAVAAR

170

A
B
C

D
E
F

ROSEMONT

Champ Des
Possibles

I

RUE

SAINT-DENIS

AVENUE

AVENUE

RUE

AVENUE

RUE

DE

DROLET

BOULEVARD

CASGRAIN

GASPÉ

MAGUIRE

HENRI-JULIEN

RUE

SAINT-DOMINIQUE

RUE

Parc Alphonse-
Télesphore-
Lépine

RUE

OUEST

SAINT-LAURENT

AVENUE FAIRMOUNT EST

AVENUE LAURIER EST

2

RUE

ÉDITIONS
DE ROBES

**CARDINAL
TEA ROOM**

SAINT-VIATEUR

AVENUE

SAINT-URBAIN

CLARK

Parc
Saint-Michel

AVENUE

RUE

AVERLY

WILENSKY'S

**BOUTIQUE
UNICORN**

MILE-END

FAIRMOUNT
BAGEL

Parc
Lahaie

**ST-VIATEUR
BAGEL**

DE

JEANNE-MANCE

L'ESPLANADE

FAIRMOUNT OUEST

**DIEU
DU CIEL!**

AVENUE

DU

3

PARC

TRESNORMALE

AVENUE

AVENUE

DE

OUEST

RUE SAINT-URBAIN

RUE

Théâtre
Fairmont

OUEST

L'ESPLANADE

OUEST

AVENUE

HUTCHISON

SAINT-JOSEPH

DUROCHER

FAIRMOUNT

VILLENEUVE

QUERBES

LAURIER

AVENUE

AVENUE

DE

L'ÉPÉE

AVENUE

AVENUE

BOULEVARD

AVENUE

DU

PARC

4

RUE

D
E
F

A
B
C

RUE
RUE
BÉLANGER

SAINT-DENIS
AVENUE
RUE
SAINT-HUBERT

1 VILLERAY
Jean-Talon

RUE
EST
DE
CHATEAUBRIAND

AVENUE HENRI-JULIEN
DROLET
LIGNE BLEUE
RUE
SAINT-VALLIER
LIGNE ORANGE

AVENUE DE
GASPÉ

CRÊPERIE
RUE
EST

LIBRAIRIE
GOURMAND

OYSTER
BAR
LES JARDINS
SAUVAGES
SAINT-DENIS

LE
POURVOYEUR
JEAN
TALON
MARKET
MARCHÉ DES
SAVEURS DU
QUÉBEC
DROLET
LA BRUME
DANS MES
LUNETTES

2
TAH-
DAH!
PASTIFICIO
SACCHETTO
MOZART
BÉLANGER
ALATI-
CASERTA

RUE SAINT-DOMINIQUE
AVENUE
DANTE
MADONNA
DELLA DIFESA
CHURCH
SAINT-ZOTIQUE
EST

PIZZERIA
NAPOLETANA
Parc
Dante

BOULEVARD
RUE
QUINCAILLERIE
DANTE
AVENUE
DE
AVENUE HENRI-JULIEN
RUE
ALMA

3
RUE
CAFFÈ
ITALIA
IMPASTO
RUE
TROU DE
BEIGNE
Parc
de Gaspé
GASPÉ

AVENUE MOZART OUEST
SAINT-LAURENT
RUE
SAINT-DOMINIQUE
AVENUE CASGRAIN

CLARK
SAINT-DOMINIQUE

RUE
Parc
Saint-Jean-
De-La-Croix

N
Parc de la
Petite-Italie
RUE BEAUBIEN EST

OUEST
SAINT-URBAIN

4
RUE SAINT-ZOTIQUE
SAINT-ZOTIQUE
ALAMBIKA
RUE BEAUBIEN OUEST

0   200 m

172
A
B
C

A B C

AUTOROUTE VILLE-MARIE

RUE SAINT-ANTOINE OUEST

AVENUE

RUE DELISLE

RUE WORKMAN

1

Parc Vinet

RUE SAINTJACQUES

Lionel-Groulx

ATWATER

RUE

JOE BEEF

■ Théâtre Corona

LIGNE VERTE

AVENUE

RUE

Parc Saint-Henri

LAPORTE

RUE

LIGNE ORANGE

OUEST

RUE CHARLEVOIX

RUE DE LÉVIS

2

ATWATER COCKTAIL CLUB

LES DOUCEURS DU MARCHÉ

DU COUVENT

AGNÈS

RUE

NOTRE-DAME

RUE

RUE ROSE-DE-LIMA

SATAY BROTHERS

BÉRARD

ATWATER MARKET

LE PARADIS DU FROMAGE

Place Saint-Henri

SAINT-HENRI

RUE SAINTE-ÉMILIE

PREMIÈRE MOISSON

HAVRE-AUX-GLACES

CANAL LOUNGE

RENTAL KAYAKS, CANOES, PEDAL BOATS

RENTAL BIKES

SAINT-AMBROISE

VINTAGE FRAMES COMPANY

RUE

RUE

Parc Louis-Cyr

SAINT-FERDINAND

RUE

Canal de Lachine

ATWATER QUAY

RUE THOMAS-KEEFER

3

RUE

SAINT-PHILIPPE

POPS ART

RUSTIQUE

SAINTE-MARGUERITE

BEAUDOIN

N ☆

Parc Sir-George-Étienne-Cartier

RUE DELINELLE

RUE DE COURCELLE

SAINT-PATRICK

15

Parc du Canal-de-Lachine

RUE

AUTOROUTE

Canal de l'Aqueduc

0   200 m

4

A B C

A   B   C

RUE VIAU

1

0   200 m

Parc Maisonneuve

RUE VIAU

N

SAPUTO STADIUM

Aréna Maurice Richard

PLANÉTARIUM RIO TINTO ALCAN

Cinéma Starcité Montréal

Viau

JAPANESE GARDEN

2

EST

Parc Olympique

JARDIN BOTANIQUE

INSECTARIUM

FIRST NATIONS GARDEN

CHINESE GARDEN

Institut National du Sport du Québec

Biodôme de Montréal

Jardin Botanique de Montréal

SHERBROOKE

GARDENS OF LIGHT TOUR STARTS

SPACE FOR LIFE

OLYMPIC STADIUM

LIGNE VERTE

DE COUBERTIN

BOULEVARD

3

AVENUE

AVENUE

PIE-IX

RUE

FOOD TRUCKS

AVENUE PIERRE DE

JEANNE-D'ARC

EST

DU MONTROYAL

D'ORLÉANS

Pie IX

RUE HOCHELAGA

AVENUE

CHÂTEAU DUFRESNE

BOULEVARD

PIE-IX

AVENUE

DU

RUE DE CHAMBLY

4

RUE RACHEL

EST

BOURBONNIÈRE

AVENUE

CHARLEMAGNE

A   B   C

A

FOOD
TRUCKS

*Parc
Olympique*

CHÂTEAU
DUFRESNE

Pie IX

LIGNE VERTE

Joliette

KITSCH À
L'OS ...
OU PAS

*Parc
Raymond-
Préfontaine*

HOCHELAGA

B

AVENUE

HOCHELAGA

RUE

AVENUE

BOULEVARD

AVENUE

HOCHELAGA

AVENUE

AVENUE

*Parc
Lalancette*

RUE AMYOT

RUE

RUE

RUE

ROUEN

DE

AYLWIN

RUE

RUE

RUE

RUE

DÉZÉRY

ADAM

DARLING

MOREAU

RUE

 RUE

ONTARIO

LETOURNEUX

DE

RUE

DESJARDINS

EST

AVENUE

NICOLET

DE

RUE

LA
FONTAINE

RUE

AVENUE

ROUEN

BENNETT

*Parc de
Rouen-Bennett*

ORIGINAL
MAISONNEUVE
MARKET

ONTARIO

TOWN-HALL-
TURNED-
LIBRARY

*Parc
Jacques-
Blanchet*

LE VALOIS

L'ESPACE
PUBLIC

ATOMIC
CAFÉ

Enfants
(swimming pool)
*Parc
Saint-
Aloysius*

CHAMBLY

JOLIETTE

Piscine Pierre-Lorange
(swimming pool)
*Parc
Hochelaga*

DAVIDSON

CUVILLIER

RUE

*Square
Dézéry*

N

MAISONNEUVE

EST

MAISONNEUVE
MARKET

PUBLIC
BATH

AVENUE MORGAN

RUE

RUE DE LA
POÉSIE

PIE-IX

COCCINELLE
JAUNE

JEANNE-D'ARC

D'ORLÉANS

BOURBONNIÈRE

VALOIS

SAINTE-CATHERINE

EST

*Parc
Édouard-
Raymond-
Fabre*

C

FONTAINE

LA

1

2

3

4

0   300 m

Fleuve Saint-Laurent

175

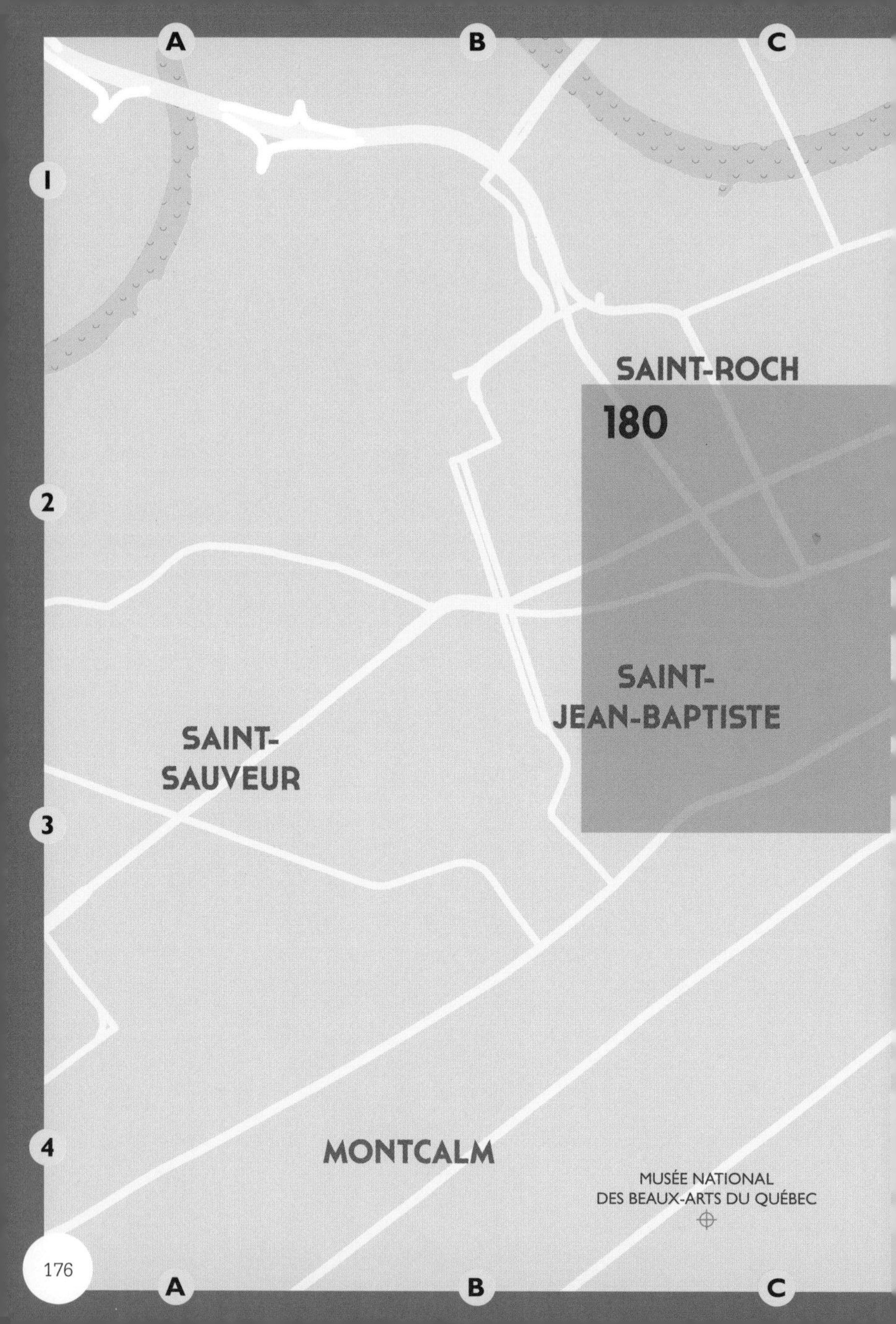

SAINT-ROCH

180

SAINT-JEAN-BAPTISTE

SAINT-SAUVEUR

MONTCALM

MUSÉE NATIONAL
DES BEAUX-ARTS DU QUÉBEC

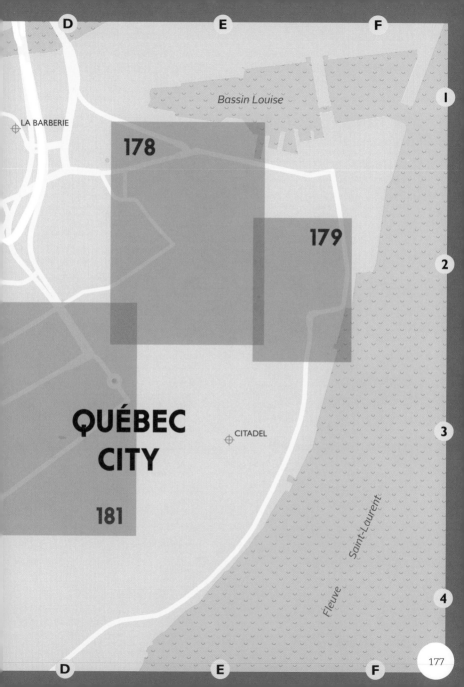

I

Bassin Louise

⊕ LA BARBERIE

178

179

2

**QUÉBEC
CITY**

⊕ CITADEL

3

181

Fleuve   Saint-Laurent

4

A B C

QUAI SAINT-ANDRÉ

MARCHÉ DU VIEUX-PORT

1

RUE SAINT-PAUL

QUAI SAINT-ANDRÉ

Hôtel Belley

Hotel Le Saint-Paul

RUE SAINT-PAUL

RUE SAINT-VALLIER EST

CÔTE DE LA CANOTERIE

RUE SAINT-THOMAS

RUE DE DINAN

RUE DES REMPARTS

CÔTE

RUE DE

AUGUSTINE MONASTERY'S RESTAURANT

RUE HAMEL

SAINT-FLAVIEN

SAINTE-FAMILLE

2

CHARLEVOIX

COUILLARD

CÔTE DU PALAIS

RUE

RUE

Parc Couillard

RUE DE L'HÔTEL-DIEU

RUE GARNEAU

RUE

MCMAHON

0   100 m

CÔTE DE LA FABRIQUE

SIMONS

Musée de l'Amérique Francophone

RUE SAINT-STANISLAS

SAINT-JEAN

RUE PIERRE-OLIVIER-CHAUVEAU

LE CHAPELIER

Basilique Cathédrale Notre-Dame-de-Québec

ELGIN

PAILLARD

Hôtel de Ville de Québec (City Hall)

Taschereau monument

3

RUE

SAINT ALEXANDRE PUB

RUE DES JARDINS

RUE DE BUADE

RUE

SAINTE-ANGÈLE

DAUPHINE

RUE COOK

RUE SAINTE-ANNE

RUE

SAINTE-ANNE

L'Homme-Rivière artwork

Auberge du Trésor (hotel)

Manoir La Salle (hotel)

Hôtel Champlain

MUSÉE DES URSULINES

RUE DES JARDINS

Le Haute Ville (hotel)

4

SAINTE-URSULE

AUX ANCIENS CANADIENS

SAINT-LOUIS

Le Manoir d'Auteuil (hotel)

Hotel Acadia

LA BUCHE

BROUSSEAU INUIT ART GALLERY

RUE

178

A B C

A | B | C

1

MUSÉE DE LA CIVILISATION

RUE

DALHOUSIE

RUE SAINT-ANTOINE

Auberge Saint-Antoine (hotel)

Cour intérieure du Petit Séminaire de Québec

RUE DES REMPARTS

RUE PORT-DAUPHIN

0   100 m

CÔTE   DE LA MONTAGNE

RUE   DU   PORCHE

2

Louis-Hébert monument

Parc Montmorency

Basilique Cathédrale Notre-Dame-de-Québec

CÔTE   DE   LA

RUE

RUE MONTAGNE

Parc de l'UNESCO

NOTRE-DAME

SAINT-PIERRE

Place de Paris

RUE DALHOUSIE

Centre Infotouriste de Québec

RUE SAINTE-ANNE

RUE DU FORT

■ Musée du Fort

Notre-Dame-des-Victoires (church)

SOUS-LE-FORT

Place d'Armes

RUE

FUNICULAIRE DU VIEUX-QUÉBEC

RUE

CHAMPLAIN

3

RUE

RUE DES TRÉSOR

RUE DU

FAIRMONT LE CHÂTEAU FRONTENAC

1608

CHAMPLAIN

TERRASSE DUFFERIN

Lorne (viewpoint)

RUE DU PETIT-CHAMPLAIN

JULES PERRIER

GARE FLUVIALE DE QUÉBEC-STQ

RUE DU PETIT-CHAMPLAIN

COCHON DINGUE

Théâtre du Petit Champlain

TERRASSE

CARRIÈRES

RUE DU MARCHÉ

TRAVERSIERS

Jardin des Gouverneurs

Victoria (viewpoint) ■

RED CANOE

RUE DES

Fleuve Saint-Laurent

4

DUFFERIN

LA PETITE CABANE À SUCRE DE QUÉBEC

RUE DU

179

A | B | C

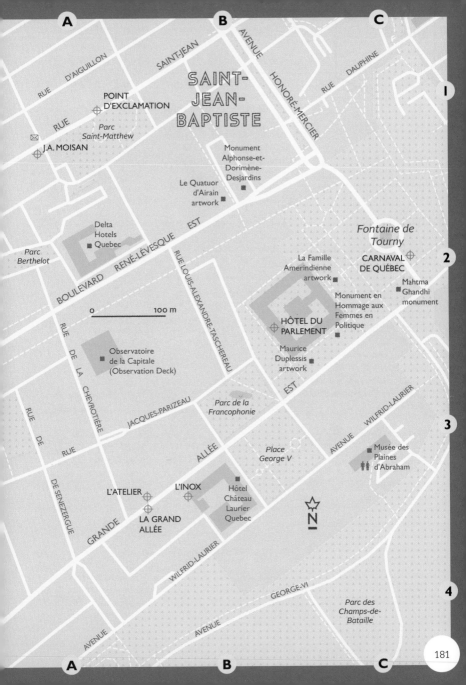

A B C

SAINT-JEAN-BAPTISTE

1

RUE D'AIGUILLON

SAINT-JEAN

AVENUE

HONORÉ-MERCIER

RUE DAUPHINE

RUE

POINT D'EXCLAMATION

Parc Saint-Matthew

J.A. MOISAN

Monument Alphonse-et-Dorimène-Desjardins

Le Quatuor d'Airain artwork

Delta Hotels Quebec

EST

RUE LOUIS-ALEXANDRE-TASCHEREAU

RUE RENÉ-LÉVESQUE

Parc Berthelot

BOULEVARD

Fontaine de Tourny

La Famille Amerindienne artwork

CARNAVAL DE QUÉBEC

Mahtma Ghandhi monument

2

Monument en Hommage aux Femmes en Politique

HÔTEL DU PARLEMENT

Maurice Duplessis artwork

0   100 m

Observatoire de la Capitale (Observation Deck)

RUE DE LA CHEVROTIÈRE

JACQUES-PARIZEAU

Parc de la Francophonie

EST

AVENUE WILFRID-LAURIER

3

ALLÉE

Place George V

RUE

RUE DE

Musée des Plaines d'Abraham

L'ATELIER

L'INOX

Hôtel Château Laurier Quebec

N

RUE DE SENEZERGUE

LA GRAND ALLÉE

GRANDE

WILFRID-LAURIER

GEORGE-VI

4

Parc des Champs-de-Bataille

AVENUE

AVENUE

A B C

INDEX

ABOUT THE AUTHOR

Melbourne writer and broadcaster Patricia Maunder lived in Montréal from 2012 to 2016. Constantly offering joys unknown in the Australian city where she was born and raised, it quickly became her other, much-loved hometown. From autumn splendour and winter wonders on her doorstep to maple beer, poutine and the world's best bagels, Montréal and its neighbours gave her much to write about, including for the city's English-language daily newspaper, *The Gazette*, and her blog, *Zut alors! An Australian in Québec*.

Returning to Melbourne as a self-proclaimed ambassador for Montréal, and Canada, she continues her media journey in travel, lifestyle and the arts. She has been a contributor to *The Sydney Morning Herald* and *The Age* in Melbourne for many years, but her contributions on three continents are many and varied, including for the Australian Broadcasting Corporation, *The Weekend Australian* and the UK's *Opera* magazine. From DJ to website editor, interviewing Booker Prize winner Margaret Atwood to driving a dogsled team, and now writing her first book, Patricia's career is an ongoing adventure.

She is a member of the Australian Society of Travel Writers and the Media, Entertainment and Arts Alliance union. Discover more at www.patriciamaunder.com.

ACKNOWLEDGEMENTS

Thanks to Melissa Kayser and Megan Cuthbert at Hardie Grant, designer Michelle Mackintosh, typesetter Megan Ellis and calm, communicative, clever project editor Alice Barker. You turned an idea into reality. Very special thanks to Montréal friends Guy L'Hérault, Paul Williams and Wilder Gonzalez for your generous support, and *merci beaucoup* to Nicola Hart and Suzanne Labrecque too. Your help and friendship, both while I was living in Montréal and during this project, are a big part of why I love this city. Thanks also to PR people Pip Macken, Andy-Riwan Gernet, Jean-Philippe Rochette, Kathy Leclerc, Nives Scott, Joanne Papineau and David Fily for your invaluable assistance. Above all, heartfelt gratitude to David Musgrave, who made the MTL experience possible in the first place, and is ever supportive of my curious career choices.

PHOTO CREDITS

Published in 2019 by Hardie Grant Travel,
a division of Hardie Grant Publishing

Hardie Grant Travel (Melbourne)
Building 1, 658 Church Street
Richmond, Victoria 3121

Hardie Grant Travel (Sydney)
Level 7, 45 Jones Street
Ultimo, NSW 2007

www.hardiegrant.com/au/travel

The maps in this publication incorporate data
© OpenStreetMap contributors.

OpenStreetMap is made available under the Open
Data Commons Open Database License (ODbL) by
the OpenStreetMap Foundation (OSMF): http://
opendatacommons.org/licenses/odbl/1.0/. Any
rights in individual contents of the database are
licensed under the Database Contents License:
http://opendatacommons.org/licenses/dbcl/1.0/

Data extracts via Geofabrik GmbH
https://www.geofabrik.de

A catalogue record for this
book is available from the
National Library of Australia

Montréal & Québec City Pocket Precincts
ISBN 9781741176247

10 9 8 7 6 5 4 3 2 1

Publisher
Melissa Kayser

Senior editor
Megan Cuthbert

Project editor
Alice Barker

Editorial assistance
Rosanna Dutson

Proofreader
Helena Holmgren

Cartographic research
Claire Johnston

Cartography
Jason Sankovic, Emily Maffei

Design
Michelle Mackintosh

Typesetting
Megan Ellis

Index
Max McMaster

Prepress
Megan Ellis and Splitting Image Colour Studio

Printed and bound in China by LEO Paper Group